STARTING STRATEGIES

STRATEGIES 1

AN INTEGRATED LANGUAGE COURSE FOR BEGINNERS OF ENGLISH

Brian Abbs
Ingrid Freebairn

Longman

Meet the peop from

ACKNOWLEDGEMENTS

Illustrators: **John Fraser** for pages: Pages 7 top and bottom left; 8; 9; 10 top; 12; 13; 16; 17; 21 bottom; 22; 24 top left; 28 top; 29 top; 32 top; 36; 37 top; 39 top; 42 top; 44 top; 47 top; 50 top; 54 top; 55; 60 top; 62 bottom; 63 top; 67; 70 top; 71 top; 76 top; 78; 80 top left; 83 top; 84 right; 89; 95; 96; 97 top; 101; 108. **Malcolm Booker** for pages: 24 middle right; 90. **Jon Davies** for pages: 37 bottom; 38 left. **Gary Rees** for pages: 39 bottom; 42 bottom; 43 bottom; 61 bottom. **Paul Ellis** for page: 49. **Teresa Cadaviera** for pages: 62 middle; 76 bottom; 80 top middle and top right. **Duncan Mil** for pages: 85 middle; 120. We are grateful to the Mansell Collection for permission to reproduce copyright photograph on page 43 top right.

Dedicated to Denis Gotobed

Pat Moaney – She's a teacher.

David Richards – He's a teacher too.

Martha Hunt – She's a doctor.

Sally B. She's journa

Longman Group Limited,
Longman House, Burnt Mill, Harlow,
Essex CM20 2JE, England
and Associated Companies throughout the world.

First published 1977
Eighth impression 1983
ISBN 0 582 51905 5

Printed in Great Britain
by Spottiswoode Ballantyne Ltd.,
Colchester and London

Contents

My name's Sally

UNIT 1

SALLY: **Mr Freeman, please.**
DOORMAN: **Yes. What's your name?**
SALLY: **Sally Baker. Miss Sally Baker. I'm from the Manchester News.**
DOORMAN: **One moment, please, Miss Baker.**
(phones)
Mr Freeman? Oh, Mr Freeman, Miss Baker is here, from the Manchester News. He's in Room One, Miss Baker.
SALLY: **Thank you.**

Set 1

Ask somebody's name
Say your name

2. Fill in your name here:

Surname: ....
First Name(s): ....
Signed: ....

1. Ask and answer like this:
What's your name?
(Peter Day)

SALLY: **Excuse me!**
MAN: **Yes?**
SALLY: **Where's Room One?**
MAN: **It's over there.**
SALLY: **Thank you.**

Set 2
Ask where places and people are
Say where places and people are

1. **Ask and answer like this:**
   Where's Kent Road?
   It's over there.
   Thank you.

   Where's........................?
   It's over there.
   Thank you.

Mr Blake

Mr Simmons

Mr Johnson

Mr Freeman

2. Ask and answer like this:

Where's Mr ....?
He's over there.
Thank you.

Miss Barnes

Miss Baker

Miss Young

Mrs Richards

3. Ask and answer like this:

Where's Mrs/Miss..................?
She's over there.
Thank you.

4. Choose a place in your town. Ask and answer like this:

Excuse me!
Yes?
Where's..................?
It's over there.
Thank you.

5. Choose a person in your classroom. Ask and answer like this:

Excuse me!
Yes?
Where's..................?
He's/She's over there.
Thank you.

9

EXTENSION

1. Write the questions in the pictures

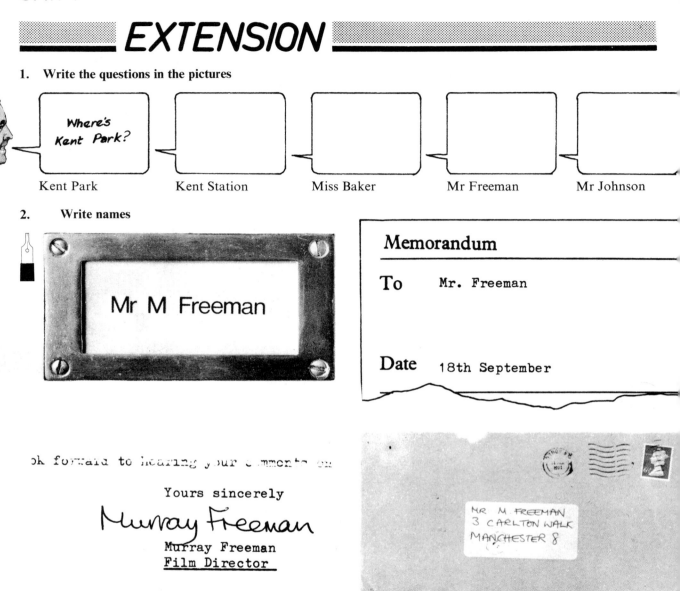

Where's Kent Park?

| Kent Park | Kent Station | Miss Baker | Mr Freeman | Mr Johnson |

2. Write names

Mr M Freeman

Memorandum

To Mr. Freeman

Date 18th September

ok forward to hearing your comments on

Yours sincerely

Murray Freeman

Murray Freeman
<u>Film Director</u>

MR M FREEMAN
3 CARLTON WALK
MANCHESTER 8

Write these names in the same way:
Sally Baker (Miss)   Tessa Richards (Mrs)
George Blake (Mr)   Your name

OPEN DIALOGUE

Talk to Murray Freeman

MURRAY: Excuse me!
STUDENT: ....
MURRAY: What's your name?
STUDENT: ....
MURRAY: Oh. My name's Murray Freeman. Where's your teacher?
STUDENT: ....
MURRAY: Oh. Thank you.

ORAL EXERCISES

1. Ask where places and people are

Kent Road
Where's Kent Road?

Mr Freeman
Where's Mr Freeman?

2. Say where people and places are (1)
Listen carefully

Where's Mr Freeman?
Mr Freeman's over there.

Where's Kent Road?
Kent Road's over there.

3. Say where places and people are (2)

Where's Kent Road?
It's over there.

Where's Mr Freeman?
He's over there.

Where's Miss Baker?
She's over there.

4. Say where people and places are (3)
Listen carefully

Where's Mr Freeman?
Mr Freeman is over there.

Where's Kent Road?
Kent Road is over there.

REMEMBER

This is how you:
1. Ask somebody's name   What's your name?
2. Say your name   (Sally Baker)
3. Ask where places and people are Where's Kent Road?
                                       Mr Freeman?
                                       Mrs Richards?

4. Say where places and people are It's
                                     He's/She's } over there
5. Attract attention   Excuse me!
6. Thank formally   Thank you.

Grammar

What's (What is)	your name?

Where's (Where is)	Kent Road? Mr Freeman? Mrs Richards?

It's (It is) He's (He is) She's (She is)	over there

Words and Phrases

a name	Mr	yes	What? (What's your name?)	your
a road	Mrs	excuse me	Where? (Where's Kent Road?)	
a park	Miss	please		
a station		thank you		
a teacher		over there		

I'm a journalist

	(Sally knocks)
MR FREEMAN:	**Come in!**
SALLY:	**How do you do, Mr Freeman. My name's Sally Baker.**
MR FREEMAN:	**Ah yes, from the Manchester News. How do you do, Miss Baker.**
	(telephone rings)
	Oh, one moment.
TESSA:	**My name's Tessa Richards. How do you do!**
SALLY:	**How do you do! I'm Sally Baker. I'm a journalist from the Manchester News. What do you do?**
TESSA:	**I'm a film director.**
SALLY:	**Oh. What does Mr Freeman do?**
TESSA:	**Murray? He's a film director too.**

Set 1

**Greet people formally
Introduce yourself**

1. Introduce yourself to your teacher, like this:

   How do you do!
My name's ....
How do you do!

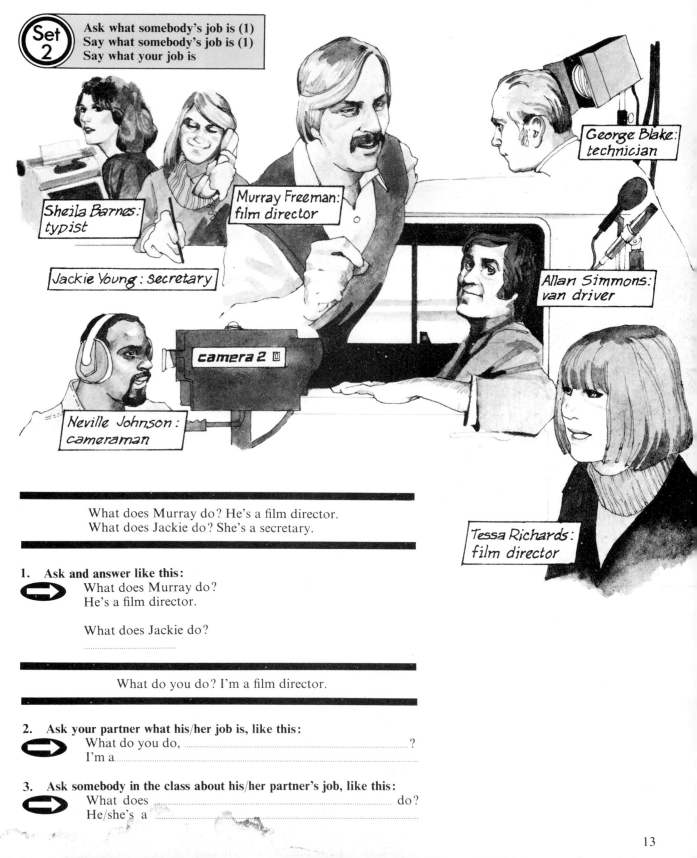

Ask what somebody's job is (1)
Say what somebody's job is (1)
Say what your job is

George Blake: technician

Sheila Barnes: typist

Murray Freeman: film director

Jackie Young : secretary

Allan Simmons: van driver

Neville Johnson: cameraman

camera 2

Tessa Richards: film director

What does Murray do? He's a film director.
What does Jackie do? She's a secretary.

1. **Ask and answer like this:**
   What does Murray do?
   He's a film director.

   What does Jackie do?
   ....

   What do you do? I'm a film director.

2. **Ask your partner what his/her job is, like this:**
   What do you do, ...?
   I'm a ....

3. **Ask somebody in the class about his/her partner's job, like this:**
   What does .... do?
   He/she's a ....

EXTENSION

A publicity brochure for Focus Films:

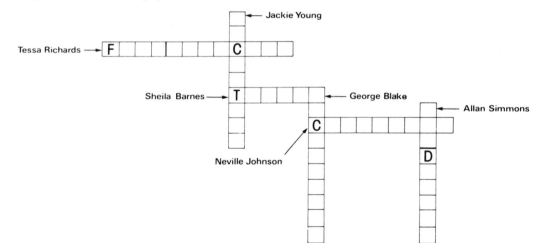

WHO'S WHO in FOCUS FILMS

Meet Murray Freeman, a film director at Focus Films: 'Hello, there, my name's Murray Freeman and I'm a film director at Focus'.

Meet Allan Simmons, a van driver: 'Hi, I'm Allan, I'm a van driver'.

Meet Tessa Richards, a film director: 'Hello, yes, I'm a film director at Focus, too'.

Meet Neville Johnson: 'I'm a cameraman'.

And George Blake: 'I'm a technician'.

And Jackie Young: 'I'm a secretary'.

WE MAKE FILMS AT FOCUS. CALL US ON THIS NUMBER **(061) 334·1564**

Word Puzzle: Guess the jobs! Don't look at page 13!

OPEN DIALOGUE

Talk to Murray Freeman

MURRAY:	Excuse me!
STUDENT:	....
MURRAY:	What's your name?
STUDENT:	....
MURRAY:	Oh, my name's Murray Freeman. How do you do!
STUDENT:	....
MURRAY:	What do you do?
STUDENT:	....
MURRAY:	Oh yes. Where's your teacher?
STUDENT:	....
MURRAY:	Oh, thank you.

ORAL EXERCISES

1. Greet the people at Focus Films formally

How do you do! My name's Murray Freeman.
How do you do, Mr Freeman.

How do you do! My name's George Blake.
How do you do, Mr Blake.

2. Ask the people at Focus Films their names, and greet them

What's your name?
Young. Miss Jackie Young.
How do you do, Miss Young.

What's your name?
Freeman. Mr Murray Freeman.
How do you do, Mr Freeman.

3. Ask about people's jobs

That's Murray over there.
What does Murray do?

That's Tessa over there.
What does Tessa do?

4. Say what the people at Focus Films do. Look at page 13

What does Murray do?
He's a film director.

What does Tessa do?
She's a film director.

REMEMBER

This is how you:
1. Greet formally — How do you do!
2. Introduce yourself — My name's Sally (Baker).
   I'm Sally Baker.
3. Ask what somebody's job is — What do you do?
   What does Murray do?
4. Say what your job is — I'm a journalist.
5. Say what somebody's job is — He's a film director.

Grammar

My name's (name is) I'm	Sally Baker Murray Freeman

I'm (I am) He's (He is) She's (She is)	a	film director journalist

What	do	you	do?
	does	Murray Tessa	

Words and Phrases

a journalist
a film director
a secretary
a technician
a cameraman
a van driver
a typist

my
too

do

How do you do!
One moment

(He's a film director too)

Hello and Goodbye!

NEVILLE: **Hello, Tessa!**
TESSA: **Hello, Neville! Neville, this is Miss Baker.**
SALLY: **Oh, please call me Sally.**
TESSA: **All right! Neville, this is Sally. Sally's a journalist.**
NEVILLE: **Hello!**
SALLY: **Hello!**
MURRAY: **Neville!**
NEVILLE: **Yes, I'm coming, Murray. Goodbye, Sally!**
SALLY: **Goodbye! Is Neville a film director?**
TESSA: **No, he isn't.**
SALLY: **What does he do?**
TESSA: **He's a cameraman.**
SALLY: **What's his name? I mean his surname?**
TESSA: **His name? Johnson, Neville Johnson.**

Set 1

Introduce people (1)
Greet informally

Look at the people in the pictures on page 13

1. **Introduce your partner to the people in the pictures, like this:**
    (Mary), this is Murray.
   (Jan), this is ....

   Neville, this is Sally. Sally's a journalist.

2. **Introduce your partner to all the people again. This time say what their jobs are too, like this:**
   (Mary), this is Murray. Murray's a film director.
   (Mary), this is .... a ....

3. **In groups of three, introduce and greet each other, like this:**
   You: (Peter), this is (Mary). (Mary)'s a ....
   (Peter): Hello!
   (Mary): Hello!

Set 2
Ask what somebody's job is (2)
Say what somebody's job is (2)

1 Sally Baker – She's a journalist.

2 Walter Moaney – He's an engineer.

3 Pat Moaney – She's a teacher.

4 David Richards – He's a teacher too.

5 Doris Blake – She's a housewife.

6 Paul Blake – . He's a student.

Maria Magnani – She's a student too.

Martha Hunt – She's a doctor.

Is Sally a journalist? Yes, she is.
Is Walter an engineer? Yes, he is.

1. Look at the people in the pictures. Ask and answer like this:

Is Sally a journalist?
Yes, she is.

Is Walter an engineer?
Yes, he is.

Is .... a(n)...................?
Yes, ...is.

Is Sally a secretary? No, she isn't.
Is Walter a technician? No, he isn't.

2. Look at the people again. Ask and answer like this:

Is Sally a secretary?
No, she isn't.

Is Walter a technician?
No, he isn't.

Is .... a(n) ....?
No, ... isn't.

Pat – doctor	Paul – engineer
David – journalist	Maria – teacher
Doris – teacher	Martha – housewife

UNIT 3

Is Neville a film director?
No, he isn't.
What does he do?
He's a cameraman.

3.   Look at the people again. Ask and answer like this:

➡   Is Sally a secretary?
No, she isn't.
What does she do?
She's ....

Is Walter a technician?
No, he isn't.
What does he do?
He's ....

Ask the questions from Exercise 2.

4.   Look at the questions in Exercise 2 again. Write the answers like this:

Sally isn't a secretary. She's a journalist.
Walter isn't a technician. He's an engineer.
Pat.............................. She's a..................

David ....
Doris ....
Paul ....
Maria ....
Martha ....

5.   Write notes on 3 people in the class, like this:

Peter Black — student
Jan White — secretary

Now write full sentences:

Peter Black is a student
Jan White is a secretary

What's his name?   What's her name?
His name's Neville. Her name's Tessa.

1.   Look at the pictures on page 13. Ask and answer like this:

➡   What's his/her name?
His/her name's ....

2.   Ask your partner about someone else in the class:

➡   What's . . .
....

EXTENSION

1. Game: Pair the names with the jobs

Allan	Neville
Sheila	Jackie
Walter	David
Tessa	Martha
George	Paul
Sally	Doris

secretary	engineer
doctor	teacher
van driver	film director
housewife	technician
student	journalist
typist	cameraman

2. **Fill in the jobs of the 4 people in the radio programme, '20 questions'**

1. Sarah Cummings, ... from Liverpool.
2. Bob Broadbent, ... from Manchester.
3. Jane Summers, ... from Manchester.
4. Mark Winters, ... from Leeds.

3. Introduce your group
Form groups of four students. Ask the other students' *names* and *jobs*.
Write them down.
Say your name and then introduce your group to the class.
The students in your group must say 'hello' or 'how do you do' when you introduce them. Start like this:

YOU: Hello! My name's (Peter). This is (Jan). She's a (secretary).
(JAN): Hello!
YOU: And this is ....

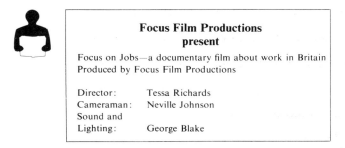

**Focus Film Productions
present**

Focus on Jobs—a documentary film about work in Britain
Produced by Focus Film Productions

Director: Tessa Richards
Cameraman: Neville Johnson
Sound and
Lighting: George Blake

OPEN DIALOGUE

You visit Focus Films with a friend. Talk to Tessa

TESSA: Hello!
STUDENT: ....
TESSA: What's your name?
STUDENT: ....
TESSA: Well, I'm Tessa. And this is Jackie. Jackie's a secretary.
JACKIE: Hello!
STUDENT: ....
TESSA: Where's your friend?
STUDENT: ....
TESSA: What's your friend's name?
STUDENT: ....
TESSA: Oh, please introduce me.
STUDENT: ....
TESSA: How do you do! Oh, here's Murray.
MURRAY: Hello!
STUDENT: ....
MURRAY: Well Tessa, it's time to start.
TESSA: Oh, all right. Well, goodbye!
STUDENT: ....

UNIT 3

ORAL EXERCISES

1. **Ask these people what their jobs are**
This is Murray.
What do you do, Murray?

This is Tessa.
What do you do, Tessa?

2. **Sally Baker asks some questions about people's jobs at Focus Films. Answer Sally's questions**
Is Murray a film director?
Yes, he is.

Is Allan a technician?
No, he isn't.

3. **Introduce people**
Introduce Neville to Murray
Murray, this is Neville.

Introduce Sally to Murray
Murray, this is Sally.

4. **Say other people's names and jobs. Look at the people on page 17**
Who's that?
Her name's Sally. She's a journalist.

Who's that?
His name's Walter. He's an engineer.

REMEMBER

This is how you:
1. Introduce people   Neville, this is Sally.
2. Say what somebody's job is   Sally's a journalist.
3. Ask what somebody's job is   Is he a film director?   What does he do?
4. Ask somebody's name   What's his/her name?
5. Say somebody's name   His/her name's................
6. Greet informally   Hello!
7. Say Goodbye   Goodbye!

Grammar

This is	Sally Baker Neville Johnson

What	do	you	do?
	does	he she	

Sally's (Sally is) Walter's (Walter is)	a an	journalist engineer

Is	he she Neville	a	film director?

Yes	he she	is
No		isn't (is not)

He	isn't	a	film director
She		an	engineer

What's (What is)	his her	name?

His Her	name's ....

Words and Phrases

an engineer	a student	a friend	his	and	this (this is Sally)	hello
a housewife	a doctor	a job	her	no	here (here's Sheila Barnes)	goodbye

Looking for a flat (1)

TOWN AND COUNTRY FLAT AGENCY Ⓣ Application Form

Name Jackie Young Mr/Mrs/Miss Occupation Secretary

Address 4, Drummond Street, Trafford Park, Manchester 17. Size of flat wanted 1 bedroom

Tel. No. Trafford Park (061) 872 4679 Offer 3 Gordon Road, Manchester 8

MAN: **Good morning! Can I help you?**

JACKIE: **Good morning! Yes. I'm looking for a small flat. One bedroom only.**

MAN: **Yes . . . just a minute. . . . What's your name, please?**

JACKIE: **Jackie Young.**

MAN: **Are you married?**

JACKIE: **No, I'm not.**

MAN: **And your address? What's your address?**

JACKIE: **4, Drummond Street, Trafford Park, Manchester 17.**

MAN: **Is that D R U double M O N D?**

JACKIE: **Yes, that's right.**

MAN: **What's your telephone number?**

JACKIE: **Trafford Park four-six-seven-nine.**

MAN: **What's the code number?**

JACKIE: **Oh-six-one eight-seven-two.**

MAN: **And what do you do, Miss Young? What's your occupation?**

JACKIE: **I'm a secretary.**

UNIT 4

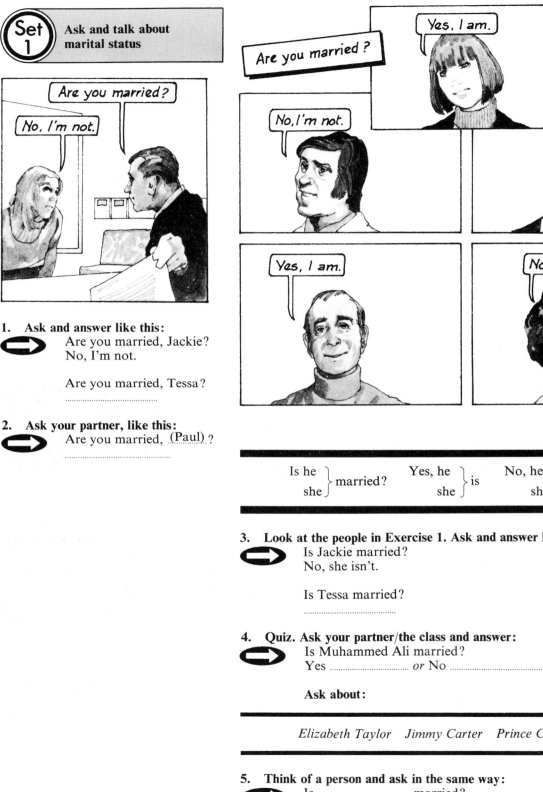

1. Ask and answer like this:

➡ Are you married, Jackie?
No, I'm not.

Are you married, Tessa?

....

2. Ask your partner, like this:

➡ Are you married, (Paul)?

....

Is he she	married?	Yes, he she	is	No, he she	isn't

3. Look at the people in Exercise 1. Ask and answer like this:

➡ Is Jackie married?
No, she isn't.

Is Tessa married?

....

4. Quiz. Ask your partner/the class and answer:

➡ Is Muhammed Ali married?
Yes .... or No ....

Ask about:

Elizabeth Taylor   *Jimmy Carter*   *Prince Charles*

5. Think of a person and ask in the same way:

➡ Is .... married?
Yes .... or No ....

Spelling

The Alphabet

Aa Bb Cc Dd Ee Ff Gg Hh Ii
Jj Kk Ll Mm Nn Oo Pp Qq Rr
Ss Tt Uu Vv Ww Xx Yy Zz

1. **Practise reading the letters in these groups of sounds**

A	B	F	Ī	O	Q	R
H	C	L	Y		U	
J	D	M			W	
K	E	N				
	G	S				
	P	X				
	T	Z				
	V					

2. **Abbreviations**
   Read these airline abbreviations

Read these abbreviations for some television and radio channels

Read these abbreviations

3. **Spelling**
   Spell your *surname* **(your last name) and the name of the street or road you live in**
   Remember **MM** = double **M**   **SS** = double **S** etc.

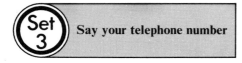 **Set 3** **Say your telephone number**

1. Say these numbers

> 507-8912 = five-oh-seven   eight-nine-one-two
> 63324   = six-double-three-two-four
> 015-9984 = ...
> 44013   = ...
> 01-286-5260 = ...

2. Ask and answer with your partner, like this:

> What's your telephone number?
> It's   four-six-seven-nine (4679)

3. Fill in this form for yourself

```
SURNAME [BLOCK CAPITALS] _____ MR/MRS/MISS/MS
MAIDEN NAME _____
FIRST NAMES _____
ADDRESS _____
TELEPHONE NUMBER _____
OCCUPATION _____
```

4. Fill in the form for your partner
Remember to ask the right questions

```
SURNAME [BLOCK CAPITALS] _____ MR/MRS/MISS/MS
MAIDEN NAME _____
FIRST NAMES _____
ADDRESS _____
TELEPHONE NUMBER _____
OCCUPATION _____
```

EXTENSION

1. Jackie applies for a job, like this:

> My name is Jackie Young and I am from Manchester,
> England. I am a secretary at Focus films. I am not married.

Now you do the same

2. **Fill in this form while you listen**

TOWN AND COUNTRY FLAT AGENCY   Application Form

Name .... Mr/Mrs/Miss   Occupation ....

Address ....   Size of flat wanted ....

Tel.No. ....   Offer ....

3. **Listen and fill in this telegram**

Counter No.		POST ✠ OFFICE	Serial No.			
Office Stamp		INLAND TELEGRAM	Charge		Chargeable Words	Sent at/by
		FOR POSTAGE STAMPS	Tariff £ excl RP			
			VAT £			
	Prefix	Handed in	Service Instructions	Actual Words	RP £	Circulation
					TOTAL £	

If you wish to pay for a reply insert RP here   **To**

BLOCK LETTERS THROUGHOUT PLEASE

CONGRATULATIONS

The particulars on the back of this form should be completed.

4. **Write the same telegram of congratulations from** you **to a** friend

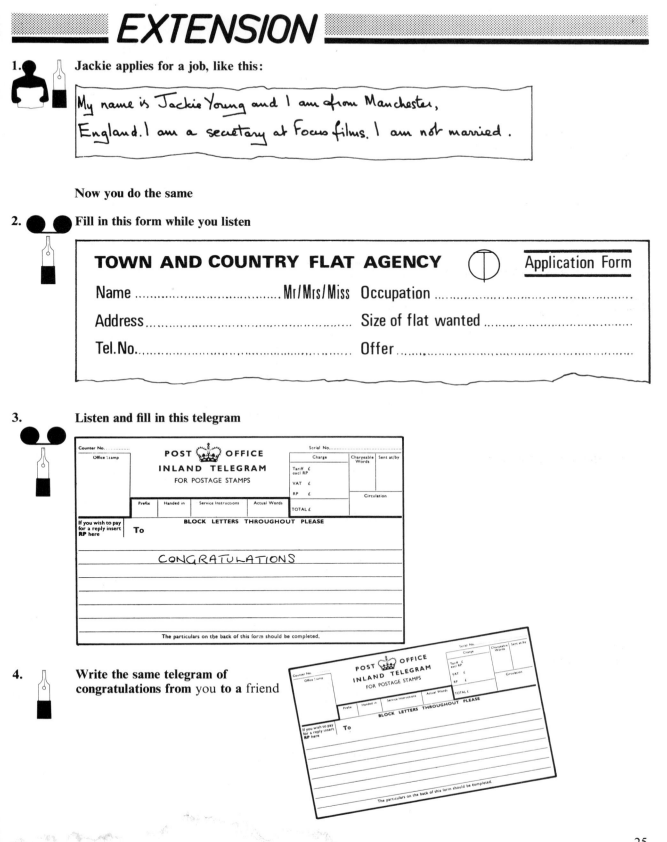

UNIT 4

5. Telephone your telegram. Your partner can be the telephone operator

TEL. OP.: Yes, can I help you?

YOU: Yes, I'd like to send a telegram please.

TEL.OP.: What is your number please?

YOU: ....

TEL. OP.: Who is the telegram to?

YOU: ....

TEL.OP.: Can you spell that please.

YOU: ....

TEL.OP.: And what is the address?

YOU: ....

TEL. OP.: Can you spell the name of the road please.

YOU: ....

TEL. OP.: And what is the message?

YOU: ....

TEL. OP.: Can you spell that please.

YOU: ....

TEL.OP.: I'll read that to you ....

YOU: Thank you. Goodbye.

TEL. OP.: Goodbye.

OPEN DIALOGUE

Talk to the man at the Flat Agency

MAN: So you want a small flat with one bedroom. I'd like some information please. What's your name?

STUDENT: ....

MAN: Can you spell that please.

STUDENT: ....

MAN: Are you married?

STUDENT: ....

MAN: And what's your address?

STUDENT: ....

MAN: And telephone number?

STUDENT: ....

MAN: Yes. And what do you do?

STUDENT: ....

MAN: Well, here's a flat – one bedroom, small, near the park *and* the station. Here's the address.

STUDENT: ....

MAN: Well, goodbye for now.

STUDENT: ....

ORAL EXERCISES

1. Spell people's names
   Look at the people on page 13
My name's Freeman
Can you spell that please.
F R double E M A N

My name's Simmons
Can you spell that please.
S I double M O N S

2. Respond to these greetings
Good morning!
Good morning!

My name's Freeman. How do you do!
How do you do!

3. Listen to the numbers, and repeat them
The code number for Manchester is 061.
061.

4. Give personal information
Are you a teacher?
No, I'm not.

Are you a student?
Yes, I am.

Is Sally married?
No, she isn't.

Is Tessa married?
Yes, she is.

Sally Baker is a journalist

Sally Baker is a journalist for the Manchester News. One day she visits Focus Films, a documentary film company in Manchester.

She meets Murray Freeman, a film director.

Murray introduces Sally to Tessa Richards. Tessa is a film director too, and is the director of a film 'Focus on Jobs'. This is a documentary film about work in Britain. The film is about people with different jobs, for example: a technician, a typist, a teacher, a housewife, a secretary and an engineer. Sally wants to write about this film for the Manchester News.

REMEMBER

This is how you:
1. Ask and talk about marital status   Are you married?
      Is he/she married?
      Yes I am/No, I'm not.
      Yes he/she is. No he/she isn't.
2. Greet somebody in the morning   Good morning!
3. Remember also how to   spell your name and address
      say your telephone number

Grammar

Are	you	married?
Is	he she	

Yes	I	am
	he she	is

No	I'm not he isn't she isn't

Words and Phrases

a flat	Good morning	one	only	send
a bedroom	Congratulations	two		
an address	married	three		
a telephone number	small	four		
a telegram		five		
a surname		six		
		seven		
		eight		
		nine		
		double		

UNIT 5

Looking for a flat (2)

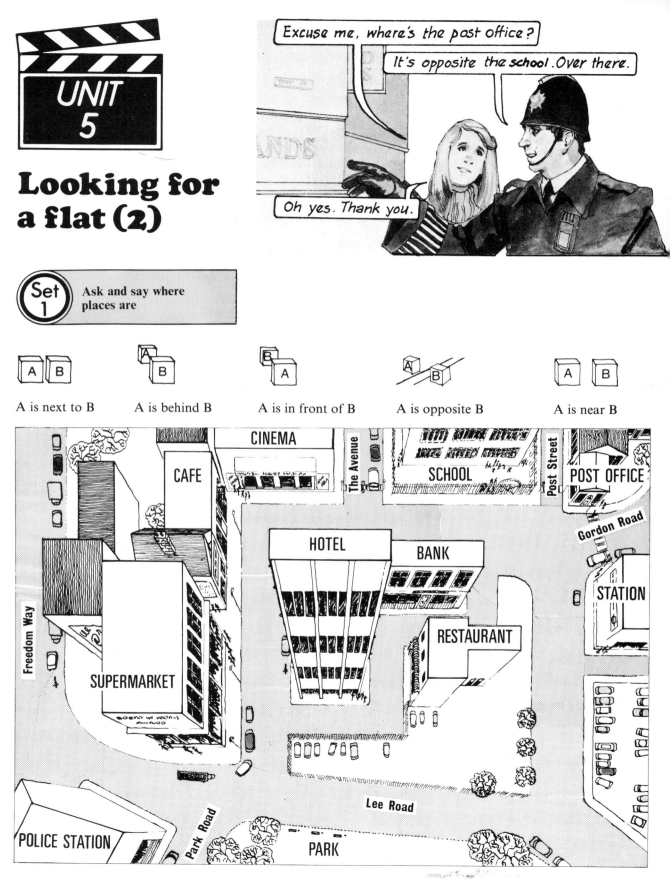

Set 1 — Ask and say where places are

A is next to B

A is behind B

A is in front of B

A is opposite B

A is near B

1. Say where places are

➡️ The post office is opposite the school

Talk about the other places in the same way

The bank/the hotel
The restaurant/the hotel
The bank/the restaurant
The school/the bank
The station/the restaurant
The park/the police station
The police station/the supermarket
The supermarket/the cafe
The hotel/the cafe

2. Ask and say where places are

➡️ Where's the post office?
It's opposite the school.
or
It's near the station.

Look at the map and ask and answer about:

the post office, the bank, the park, the station, the police station, the cinema.

3. Draw a map of part of your town. Write in the names of the streets, mark the bank etc.
With a partner, ask and answer as in Exercise 2.

4. Memory Game
Look at the map for one minute. Then shut your book and say where places are. How many can you remember? Your partner can help you.

5. Word Game
What are these places? Write them down.
1. MICANE   4. TASTNIO
2. NAKB   5. HOLOSC
3. LTOEH   6. ETASUNRRTA

What do you do Miss Young?

I'm a secretary.

MAN:	**What do you do Miss <u>Young</u>?**
JACKIE:	**I'm a <u>secretary.</u>**
MAN:	**Oh, a <u>secretary.</u>**
JACKIE:	**That's right.**
MAN:	**Where?**
JACKIE:	**At <u>Focus Films.</u>**
MAN:	**I see.**
JACKIE:	**I'm looking for a small <u>one</u>-bedroom flat near my office.**
MAN:	**Now let's see. Ah yes, here's one.**
	It's in <u>Gordon Road.</u> Yes, and it's a <u>one</u>-bedroom flat.
JACKIE:	**<u>Gordon Road</u>? Where is <u>Gordon Road</u> exactly?**
MAN:	**Here, look at the map. <u>Gordon Road</u> is here, <u>next to</u> the <u>station.</u>**
JACKIE:	**That's good.**
MAN:	**Yes. Well here's the address and the telephone number: 3, <u>Gordon Road, Manchester 8. 334 8956.</u>**
JACKIE:	**Thank you very much. Goodbye.**
MAN:	**Goodbye.**
MAN:	**Hello, hello! <u>334 8956</u>? Oh, good, <u>Mrs Parker</u>?**
(phones)	**A <u>young woman</u> is coming to see the flat. <u>Jackie Young.</u> Yes, that's right. <u>She's a secretary at Focus Films.</u> Oh, <u>no, she isn't married.</u> Yes. Good, good, <u>she's</u> very nice. Thank you <u>Mrs Parker.</u> Goodbye.**

Read the dialogue again with a partner. Say what you do. and offer a flat from the list below.

Town and Country Flat Agency

① 7 LEE ROAD
1 bedroom (woman preferred)
Tel:(061) 334 4379
    Mrs Galloway

② 6b FREEDOM WAY
1 bedroom (man preferred)
Tel:(061) 334 2091
    Miss Robson

③ 9 THE AVENUE
2 bedrooms
Tel:(061) 334 3981
    Mrs Jones

④ 3 GORDON ROAD
1 bedroom (man or woman)
Tel:(061) 334 8956
    Mrs Parker

EXTENSION

1. Jackie's mother, Mrs Young, is in Manchester. She wants to see Jackie for lunch. Jackie writes her a message

> Mother
>
> Please meet me outside the cafe. You can't miss it.
> It's next to the ABC cinema.
>
> — Jackie

Now write a message like this to a friend. Choose a place to meet on the map on page 28. Say where it is

2. Listen to the tape and say where you are. There are five different places

1. I'm in a ....
2. I'm at a ....
3. I'm in a ....
4. I'm in a ....
5. I'm in a ....

OPEN DIALOGUE

You are at the station on the map. A stranger talks to you

STRANGER: Excuse me!

STUDENT: ....

STRANGER: Can you help me. I'm looking for the bank. Where is it?

STUDENT: ....

STRANGER: Oh, is it? Thank you. And then can you tell me – is the cinema near the bank?

STUDENT: ....

STRANGER: Oh, good. Well, thank you very much. Goodbye.

STUDENT: ....

Jackie Young Goes to a Flat Agency

Jackie Young is a new secretary at Focus Films, the documentary film company in Manchester.

Jackie is from Trafford, a suburb of Manchester, but she wants a flat near her job at Focus Films. She wants a small one-bedroom flat and she wants a nice landlady or landlord. She goes to a flat agency.

The man at the 'Town and Country Flat Agency' gives Jackie the address of a one-bedroom flat in Gordon Road, next to the station. The name of the landlady is Mrs Parker. The man telephones Mrs Parker and gives her Jackie's name and some information about her.

ORAL EXERCISES

1. Ask where places are
Ask the policeman where the bank is.
Excuse me, where's the bank?

Ask the policeman where the post office is.
Excuse me, where's the post office?

2. Say where places are. Look at the map on page 28
Excuse me, can you help me?
Is the bank next to the hotel?
Yes. That's right. Next to the hotel.

Is the post office opposite the school?
Yes. That's right. Opposite the school.

3. Say where places are again. Help the tourist
Excuse me, where's the bank?
It's next to the hotel.

Excuse me, where's the post office?
It's opposite the school.

4. Answer the questions
Is the school opposite the bank or the hotel?
It's opposite the bank.

Is the cinema near the school or the restaurant?
It's near the school.

5. Say the correct places. Look at the map again
Is the bank opposite the park?
No, it isn't, it's opposite the school.

Is the school opposite the hotel?
No, it isn't, it's opposite the bank.

REMEMBER

This is how you:
1. Say goodbye formally   Goodbye!
2. Ask and say where places are   Where's the bank?
       It's next to the station.
3. Thank somebody   Thank you very much.

Grammar

Where's	the	bank? post office? cinema?

It's	next to behind in front of opposite near	the	station park hotel

Words and Phrases

a post office	an office	next to	young	or	want
a school		behind	nice		
a bank	a woman	in front of			
a hotel	a man	opposite			
a restaurant		near			
a police station					
a supermarket					
a cinema		thank you very much			
a café		I don't know			
a map					

Consolidation Unit

At the tourist information desk at Manchester Airport

TOURIST:	**Excuse me!**
GIRL:	**Yes, can I help you?**
TOURIST:	**I'm looking for a <u>hotel.</u>**
GIRL:	**Yes. In the centre or near the airport?**
TOURIST:	<u>**In the centre.**</u>
GIRL:	**Cheap or expensive?**
TOURIST:	<u>**It doesn't matter.**</u>
GIRL:	**Let's see . . . here's one. <u>The Grand Hotel.</u>**
TOURIST:	**Where is it?**
GIRL:	**It's opposite the Bus <u>Station.</u>**
TOURIST:	**I see. What's the address?**
GIRL:	**It's <u>the Grand Hotel, Aytoun Street, Manchester 1.</u>**
TOURIST:	**And the telephone number?**
GIRL:	<u>**236 9559.** </u>**But I'll telephone for you.**
TOURIST:	**Thank you very much.**
GIRL:	**What is your name, please?**
TOURIST:	<u>**Gillett. Mr Frank Gillett.**</u>
GIRL:	**Can you spell it please.**
TOURIST:	<u>**G I double L E double T.**</u>
GIRL:	**Thank you. One moment, <u>Mr Gillett.</u>**
	(dials)
	Hello! <u>Grand Hotel?</u> Can I reserve a room for a <u>Mr Gillett</u> for tonight please. Yes. Thank you. Goodbye. That's all right, <u>Mr Gillett.</u>
TOURIST:	**Thank you very much. Oh, where are the taxis?**
GIRL:	**They're over there.**
TOURIST:	**Thank you.**

1. **Read the dialogue with a partner. Give your name and spell it.**

2. **Look at the Tourist Information Service Guide. Choose** *two* **of the following situations and practise the dialogue again with your partner.**
   – you want a fairly cheap hotel near the airport
   – you want an expensive restaurant in the centre
   – you are a student and you want a cheap room at a hostel in the centre
   – you want a cheap restaurant near the airport
   – you are on a camping holiday
   Note: you reserve a *room* at a hotel or a hostel
              table at a restaurant

3. ●● **Listen to the dialogue again. This time it is slightly different.**

4. **Now choose a place to stay in Manchester and complete the Registration Form.**

Registration

Surname: ....

First Name(s): ....

Country: ....

Home Address: ....

....

Tourist Address in Manchester: ....

....

Telephone Number: ....

MANCHESTER AIRPORT TOURIST INFORMATION SERVICE				
HOTELS				
NAME	Grand Hotel	Hotel Piccadilly	Excelsior Hotel	Tatton Arms Hotel
ADDRESS	Aytoun Street Manchester 1	Piccadilly Plaza Manchester 1	Wythenshawe Manchester 22	Mill Lane Northenden Manchester 22
TELEPHONE	(061) 236 9559	(061) 236 8414	(061) 437 5811	(061) 998 4750
POSITION	In the centre opposite to the bus station	In the centre near the bus station	Near the airport opposite the car park	Near the airport and near M6 motorway
PRICE for single room	£12.20	£16.25	£11.50	from £3.00
RESTAURANTS				
NAME	WHEELS	THE KNIFE AND FORK	MULLIGANS	THE PICCADILLY
ADDRESS	5, Whitworth Street Manchester 1	9, London Road Manchester 1	Wythenshawe Manchester 22	67, Princess Street Manchester 1
TELEPHONE	675 8859	678 0576	673 8876	674 9054
POSITION	In the centre next to the Palace Theatre	In the centre opposite Piccadilly Station	Near the airport	In the centre near the air terminal
CATEGORY	★★★★	★★★★	★★	★

HOSTEL AND STUDENT ACCOMMODATION		
NAME	NATIONAL UNION OF STUDENTS (N.U.S.) HOSTEL	YOUNG MEN'S AND WOMEN'S CHRISTIAN ASSOCIATION (Y.M.C.A.) (Y.W.C.A.) HOSTEL
ADDRESS	2, Lever Street Manchester 1	6, Blackfriars Street Manchester 1
TELEPHONE	675 4329	657 0045
POSITION	In the centre opposite Piccadilly Gardens	In the centre next to the ABC Cinema

CAMPING SITES		
NAME	Blue Skies	Cosmos
ADDRESS	Blackhills Manchester 9	River Road Manchester 7
TELEPHONE	986 3345	895 4396
POSITION	Next to the river outside the city	Near the airport behind the Sports Stadium

Welcome to the Elizabeth Hotel!

FOR YOUR INFORMATION

The address of the hotel is: The Elizabeth Hotel,

St. Anne's Square,

Manchester 1.

The telephone number of the hotel is:

Manchester
(Code: 061) 675 9500

YOUR ROOM NUMBER IS: *Room 16*

The manager of the hotel is: Dennis Hickling

The hotel is in the centre of the city near the river.
It is behind the Royal Theatre and near the ABC Cinema.
The new shopping centre is opposite the hotel.

ALSO AT YOUR SERVICE

The Elizabeth Coffee Bar and Restaurant

The Express Self-Service Cafeteria

The Elizabeth Sauna

The King and Queen Bar

The Number 7 Cocktail Bar and Lounge

The Elizabeth Boutique

Breakfast   07.00 - 10.00

Lunch   12.00 - 14.00

Dinner   19.00 - 21.00

Enjoy your stay at the Elizabeth and
please
REMEMBER TO LEAVE YOUR KEY!

5. You are on holiday in Manchester. You are staying at the Royal Hotel. You meet Jackie Young in the hotel lobby and talk to her.

Put the right questions in the gaps

STUDENT:	Hello!
JACKIE:	Hello!
STUDENT:	*What's your name?*
JACKIE:	Jackie.
STUDENT:	....
JACKIE:	Young. My name's Jackie Young.
STUDENT:	....
JACKIE:	No, I'm not.
STUDENT:	....
JACKIE:	I'm a secretary.
STUDENT:	....
JACKIE:	That's right!
STUDENT:	....
JACKIE:	At Focus Films.
STUDENT:	Oh yes!..........................
JACKIE:	Over there opposite the Reception Desk
STUDENT:	....
JACKIE:	Mmmm. Yes, please.
STUDENT:	Here you are.
JACKIE:	Thank you very much.

Coffee?
What's your name?
Here in Manchester?
What do you do?
Are you a tourist?
What's your surname?
Where do you work?
Where's the Coffee Bar?

Now work with your partner again and meet these people

NAME	Tessa Richards	Martha Hunt	Pat Moaney
OCCUPATION	film director	doctor	teacher
PLACE OF WORK	Focus Films	Manchester Royal Infirmary	Kent Road School

6. **Fill in the right words in the gaps.**

A. What's your n _ _ _ please?
B. Allan Simmons.
A. And your a _ _ _ _ _ _ ?
B. 9, Broad Street, Manchester.
A. And what is your t - - - - - - - n - - - - - ?
B. 654 3214.
A. What's the c _ _ _ number for Manchester?
B. 061.
A. Are you m _ _ _ _ _ _ ?
B. No, I'm not.
A. And what do you do?
B. I'm a v _ _ _ _ _ _ _ _ .
A. And you want a f _ _ _ ?
B. Yes, that's right. A one b _ _ _ _ _ _ f _ _ _ .
A. Where do you want it?
B. In the centre near the s _ _ _ _ _ _ .
A. Right, let's see, yes here's a flat.

7. **Rewrite these words in groups of 4 words**

behind   nine
two   school
technician   good morning
hello   doctor
secretary   five

near   engineer
park   bank
opposite   next to
eight   station
goodbye   how do you do

REMEMBER

Words and Phrases

a centre	fairly	reserve
an airport	expensive	remember
an air terminal	cheap	work
a car park	outside	
a hostel		
a shopping centre		
a price		
a room	a bus	
a table	a river	
a taxi	a country	
a tourist	a bar	

UNIT 7

ALLAN: **Morning, girls!**
TESSA: **Oh, good morning Allan. Jackie, meet Allan. He's a van driver. Allan, this is Jackie, our new secretary.**
ALLAN: **Hello, Jackie!**
JACKIE: **Hello, Allan!**
ALLAN: **Are you English, Jackie?**
JACKIE: **No, I'm not.**
ALLAN: **Where are you from?**
JACKIE: **Guess!**

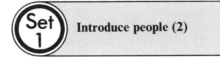

Set 1   Introduce people (2)

Jackie, meet Allan. He's a van driver.

---

1. Look at the people on page 13. Introduce all the people to Jackie, like this:

    Jackie, meet Murray.   He's a film director.
Jackie, meet .... She's a ....

2. Introduce your partner to somebody in the class, like this:

    You: (Peter), meet (Mary) She's (He's) a ....
(Mary):   Hello (Peter)
(Peter):   Hello (Mary)

Set 2 Ask and talk about nationality

ALLAN: **Are you American?**
JACKIE: **No, I'm not.**
ALLAN: **Er… are you Canadian?**
JACKIE: **No, I'm not.**
ALLAN: **Well, are you Irish?**
JACKIE: **No, I'm not. I'm Australian.**
ALLAN: **Australian!**
JACKIE: **That's right. I'm from Melbourne, Australia. I'm Australian. My father's Australian but my mother's English. Where are you from, Allan?**
ALLAN: **I'm from London.**

1. **Say what nationality you are and write it down**

     I'm ....

2. **Ask three people in the class if they are the same nationality as you, like this:**

Are you ....?
Yes, I am *or*
No, I'm not. I'm ....

She's Canadian   He's English   They're Australian   They're American

Look at the people in picture (iv)

Are they Canadian?   No, they aren't.
Are they American?   Yes, they are.

3. **Look at the people in the four pictures and ask and answer these questions:**

Picture (i)   Is she English?
                No, she .... She's ....
Picture (ii)   Is he Irish?
                ....
Picture (iii)   Are they American?
                ....
Picture (iv)   Are they Canadian?
                ....

4. Look at the pictures. Ask and answer like this:

⮕ Picture (i)
Is she American?

No, she isn't.
She's English.
Look at her car.

Picture (ii)
Is he Irish?

....

Picture (iii)
Are they American?

....

Picture (iv)
Are you English?

....

Picture (v)
Are you Canadian?

....

5. Word Game.

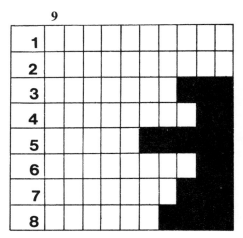

Clues

1. Car plate AUS. This man is
   ....
2. Focus Films is in .... (town in England)
3. My brother and sister are from London. They're ....
4. Tessa's surname is ....
5. Car plate IRL. They're ....
6. He's from Montreal. He's
   ....
7. My .... is 3, Gordon Road.
8. My .... is 651 4321.

When you have done these 8 clues you can see the last word, number 9 down. Write down what this word is here:

Set 3   **Ask and say where people are from**

Where are you from?

I'm from London.

1.   **Ask three people in the class where they are from, like this:**

➡️   Where are you from?   I'm from ....

Ask and say where other people in the class are from, like this:

➡️   Where is (Peter) from?   He's/She's from...............................

1   Liz & David — We're from Manchester / Manchester

2   Sue & John — We're from Melbourne / Melbourne

3   Carol & Steve — We're from Liverpool / Liverpool

4   Judy & Michael — We're from England / ENGLAND

5   Angela & Gary — We're from America / U.S.A

6   Janet & Don — We're from Canada / CANADA

---

i)   Are you from London? No, we aren't. We're from Manchester.
ii)   Are you from Sydney? No, we aren't. We're from Melbourne.
iii)   Are you from Liverpool? Yes, we are.

---

2.   **Look at the people in the pictures. Ask and answer like this:**

    Are you from .... ?
   Yes, we are. *or* No, we aren't. We're from ....

---

i)   Are they from London? No, they aren't. They're from Manchester.
ii)   Are they from Melbourne? Yes, they are.

---

3.   **Ask and answer again about the people like this:**

    Are they from .... ?
   Yes, they are, *or* No, they aren't. They're from ....

39

EXTENSION

1. Listen to the four people singing. What country are they from? Choose from: ENGLAND, AMERICA, AUSTRALIA, IRELAND, and write in your answers here.

Song One: ....

Song Two: ....

Song Three: ....

Song Four: ....

OPEN DIALOGUE

Bill, an American boy, comes to see you at school. Talk to him

BILL: Hi! My name's Bill.
STUDENT: ....
BILL: Oh, are you English?
STUDENT: ....
BILL: Oh, where are you from? Which town?
STUDENT: ....
BILL: Oh well, I'm from New York City, in the United States. Say, is your teacher English?
STUDENT: ....
BILL: Well, I must go. Goodbye.
STUDENT: ....

ORAL EXERCISES

1. Say where you are from. You are the people in the pictures on page 39
Liz and David – Where are you from?
We're from Manchester. Where are you from?

2. Give correct information about where people are from. Look at the pictures again
Are Liz and David from London?
No, they aren't. They're from Manchester.

Are Sue and John from Liverpool?
No, they aren't. They're from Melbourne.

3. Confirm people's nationality
Is he English?
Of course he's English. Look at his car.

Is she American?
Of course she's American. Look at her car.

4. Spell the names of countries
Spell Canada
CANADA

The People of Britain
Many people living and working in Britain are not British. Two people at Focus Films are not British – Jackie Young is an Australian secretary, and Neville Johnson is a Jamaican cameraman. But Australia and Jamaica are English-speaking countries, so it is easy for Jackie and Neville to live and work in Britain.

Many people come to live and work in Britain from non-English speaking countries in Europe, Africa and Asia. It is not so easy for European, African and Asian people to live and work in Britain if they cannot speak English. It is also not so easy for their children to study in British schools.

5. **Say what nationality people are. Look at the pictures on page 39**
   Sue and Larry are from Washington. They're American.
   Picture (i)   What about the people from Manchester?
                 They're English.
   Picture (ii) What about the people from Melbourne?
                 They're Australian.

6. **Say where places are**
   Where's Sydney?
   It's in Australia.

   Where's Liverpool?
   It's in England.

REMEMBER

This is how you:

1. Introduce people

   Jackie, meet Allan.
   He's a van driver.

2. Ask and talk about nationality

   Are you English?
   Yes, I am/No, I'm not. I'm Australian.
   Are they Canadian?
   Yes, they are/No, they aren't. They're ....

3. Ask and say where people are from

   Where are you from?
   I'm from Melbourne.
   Are you from London?
   Yes, we are/No, we aren't.

4. Say you must leave

   I must go!

Grammar

Are	you they	English?
Is	he she	from England?

Yes	I	am
	we they	are are
	he she	is is

No	I'm	not
	we they	aren't aren't
	he she	isn't isn't

I'm We're They're He's She's	American from America

Look at	my your his her our their	car!

where	are	you	from?
	is	he she	

I'm He's She's	from	Liverpool Manchester Australia

Words and Phrases

a car	Manchester	English	England	from (I'm from . . .)	meet
a girl	London	American	America	that's right	guess
a boy	Liverpool	Canadian	Canada	I must go!	look at
a father	Melbourne	Irish	Ireland	not (I'm not (Irish))	
a mother	Sydney	Australian	Australia	of course	
a brother	New York City				
a sister					
		new	our		
		easy	their		
		many			

Where exactly do you live?

I live in Trafford.

Allan Simmons is still talking to Jackie.

JACKIE: **Where do you live? I mean, where do you live now?**
ALLAN: **I'm from London, but I live in Manchester now.**
JACKIE: **I live in Trafford.**
ALLAN: **Trafford?**
JACKIE: **It's a suburb west of Manchester.**
ALLAN: **Oh yes, that's right.**

Set 1 Ask where people live
Say where you live

Where do you live?
I live in Trafford.

---

1. **Look at the single people on the map. Ask and answer like this:**
 Where do you live, (Jane)?
I live in (Manchester).

2. **Now ask you partner:**
 Where do you live, ...?
I live in ....

Where do you live?
We live in London.

---

3. **Look at the couples on the map. Ask and answer like this:**
 Where do you live, Mr and Mrs Ace?
We live in London.

Where do they live?
They live in London.

---

4. **Look at the couples again. Ask and answer like this:**
 Where do Mr and Mrs Ace live?
They live in London.

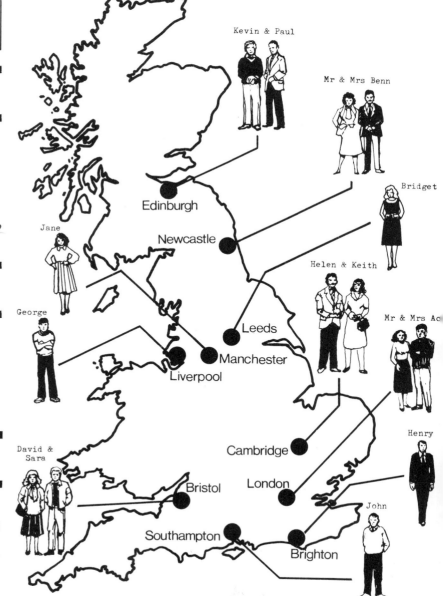

Kevin & Paul

Mr & Mrs Benn

Bridget

Edinburgh

Jane

Newcastle

Helen & Keith

George

Leeds

Mr & Mrs Ace

Manchester

Liverpool

Henry

David & Sara

Cambridge

London

Bristol

John

Southampton

Brighton

Set 2 — Ask and say where people live exactly

Where do you live? I live in the north of England.

1. **Look at the map on page 42 again. Ask the people from Brighton, Newcastle, Bristol and Cambridge where they live, like this:**

Where do you live, Henry?
I live in the .... of England.

2. **Ask your partner where he/she lives, like this:**

Where do you live, ...?
I live in the .... of ....

Where exactly do they live? They live in a suburb of London.

3. **Look at the people from London, Newcastle, Edinburgh, Bristol and Cambridge. These people live in the suburbs of these cities. Ask and answer about them like this:**

Where do Mr and Mrs Ace live?
They live in a suburb of London.

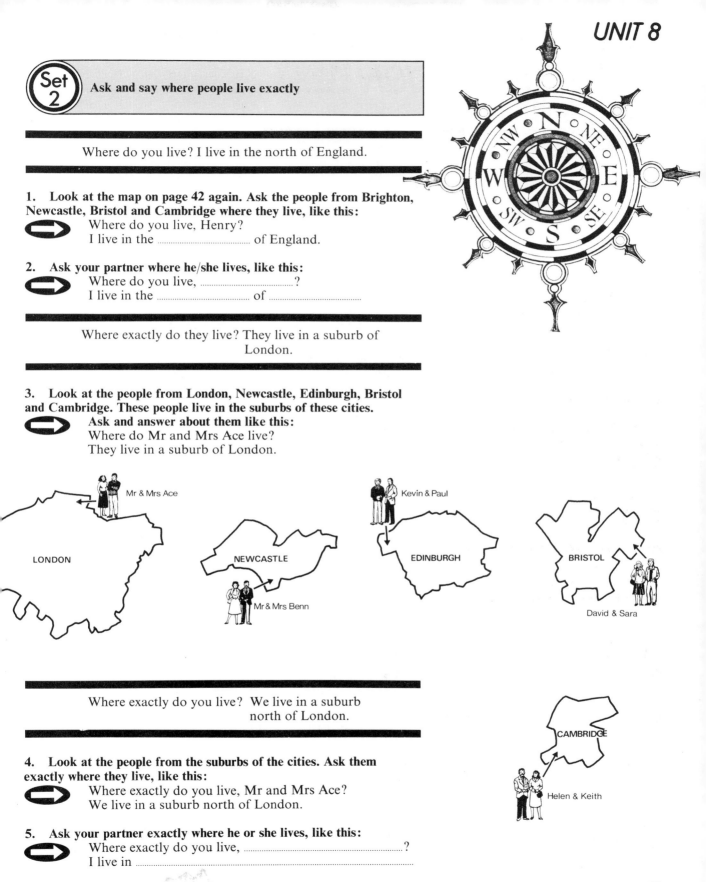

Mr & Mrs Ace
LONDON
NEWCASTLE
Mr & Mrs Benn
Kevin & Paul
EDINBURGH
BRISTOL
David & Sara
CAMBRIDGE
Helen & Keith

Where exactly do you live? We live in a suburb north of London.

4. **Look at the people from the suburbs of the cities. Ask them exactly where they live, like this:**

Where exactly do you live, Mr and Mrs Ace?
We live in a suburb north of London.

5. **Ask your partner exactly where he or she lives, like this:**

Where exactly do you live, ...?
I live in ....

EXTENSION

1. FOCUS MAGAZINE | NEW STAFF

Meet our new
secretary,
Jackie Young.
Here's Jackie

"Hello! My name's
Jackie Young. I'm 20.
I'm a secretary at Focus
Films. I'm Australian
but I live in England
now. I live with my
parents in Trafford,
a suburb west of
Manchester. But I want
a flat near Focus Films".

2. Imagine that you are a new student in your class. Write a few lines
like this about yourself for a class magazine (give the magazine a
name)

3. Listen to Jackie talking to Allan Simmons again

4. Listen to the interview with Sally Maxwell and fill in her
application form for the programme

intervening clutter of an Oriental
port. Its unfamiliarity did not frighten
me. After all, my father was Colonial
Secretary, acting Governor. I'd settle

Every morning a little starched
white dress was laid out on my bed
and I was driven down the drive to
the Zenana Mission School by my
own chauffeur, an exuberant up-

the bell again and with the same
quietness and a remarkable speed,
someone would come and break its
neck.

When it grew cooler I liked to

unique rubbery stench of the Singa-
pore River that I missed most, and
I miss it still●

*Next week: Sir Monty Finniston on
Glasgow.*

NAME OF PROGRAMME:

Guess the Nationality Quiz

PROGRAMME LEADER:

Don Bakersfield

If you would like to be on our programme, please fill in the following form:

Name: _____ Mr/Mrs/Miss

Nationality: _____

Place of Birth: _____
(town and country)

Present Address: _____
(town and country)

Occupation: _____

Signed: *Sally Maxwell*

OPEN DIALOGUE

Talk to Allan Simmons

ALLAN: Hello, I'm Allan, Allan Simmons. What's your name?
STUDENT: ....
ALLAN: Are you a student?
STUDENT: ....
ALLAN: Are you English?
STUDENT: ....
ALLAN: Oh, well, *I'm* English. I'm from the south of England. London, actually. What about you? Where are you from?
STUDENT: ....
ALLAN: Really! I live in Manchester now. Where do you live?
STUDENT: ....
ALLAN: And your parents? Where do they live?
STUDENT: ....
ALLAN: Where is that exactly?
STUDENT: ....
ALLAN: Oh, yes. Well, I must go now. Goodbye for now!
STUDENT: ....

Towns and Cities in Britain

Sheila Barnes is a typist at Focus Films. She lives in Manchester. Manchester is a big city in the north west of England.

In fact, Sheila comes from Bolton. Bolton is a medium size town north west of Manchester, and Sheila's parents still live there. But life is not very interesting in Bolton for young people like Sheila. There is not much work and there is not much to do. So Sheila lives and works in Manchester now and visits her parents at weekends.

ORAL EXERCISES

1. Say where you live. You are the people in the pictures on page 43

Mr and Mrs Ace, do you live in London?
Well, we live in a suburb of London.

Mr and Mrs Benn, do you live in Newcastle?
Well, we live in a suburb of Newcastle.

2. Say exactly where people live. Look at page 43

Mr and Mrs Ace live in a suburb of London.
Yes, in a suburb north of London.

Mr and Mrs Benn live in a suburb of Newcastle.
Yes, in a suburb south of Newcastle.

3. Show interest and ask exactly where people live.

We're from the north of England.
Oh, I'm from the north too. Where exactly do you live?

We're from the south of Canada.
Oh, I'm from the south too. Where exactly do you live?

4. Say where places are

Where's Newcastle exactly?
It's in the north of England.

Where's Southampton exactly?
It's in the south of England.

5. Say exactly where people live. Look at the pictures on page 43 again.

Where exactly do Mr and Mrs Ace live?
They live north of London, in a suburb.

Where exactly do Mr and Mrs Benn live?
They live south of Newcastle, in a suburb.

UNIT 8

REMEMBER

This is how you:

1. Ask and say where people live

Where do you live?
Where do they live?
I live in London.
We/They live in Leeds.

2. Ask and say where people live exactly

Where do you live?
Where exactly do they live?
I live in a suburb (north) of London.
We/They live in the north of England.

Grammar

Where	do	you they	live?

I We they	live	in	London England		
			the	north south	of England
			a suburb of	London Manchester	
			a suburb	north south	of	London Manchester

Words and Phrases

a suburb	Brighton	north	now	live
parents	Newcastle	south	but	
	Edinburgh	east	exactly	
	Bristol	west	in	
	Leeds			
	Southampton		what about?	
	Cambridge			

One bed, one sit, K&B

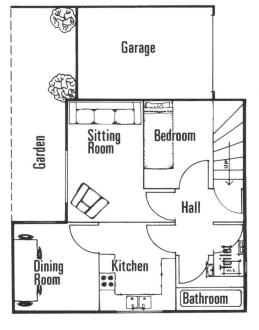

How do you do! I'm Jackie Young. I'm from the Town and Country Flat Agency.

Oh yes, the Flat Agency. Come in. The flat's upstairs.

Thank you.

Jackie goes to see the flat in Gordon Road. Mrs Parker opens the door.

JACKIE:	How do you do! I'm Jackie Young. I'm from the Town and Country Flat Agency.
MRS PARKER:	Oh yes, the Flat Agency. Come in. The flat's upstairs.
JACKIE:	Thank you.
MRS PARKER:	This is the bedroom.
JACKIE:	Yes.
MRS PARKER:	And that's the sitting room.
JACKIE:	Mmm! It's nice and big. Is this the bathroom?
MRS PARKER:	Yes, it is.
JACKIE:	Oh! It isn't very big. Is this the kitchen?
MRS PARKER:	No, it isn't. That's the kitchen over there. This is the toilet.
JACKIE:	Oh, I see. Well, thank you very much.
MRS PARKER:	That's all right.

Set 1   **Show and ask about places**

This is the bedroom and that's the sitting room.

Look at the plan of the flat

1. **Show your partner the different places like this:**

⟹   This is the bedroom and that's the sitting room
     This is the bathroom and that's the bedroom

        hall/sitting room
        kitchen/dining room
        bedroom/kitchen
        bathroom/toilet
        garage/garden

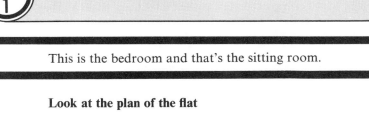

Is this the bathroom?
Yes, it is.

2. Look at the flat again and ask and answer about the places like this:

 Is this the ....?
Yes, it is.

Is this the kitchen?
No, it isn't. That's the kitchen over there.

3. Look at the flat and ask and answer about the places like this:

 Is this the ....?
No, it isn't. That's the ....
.........................over there.

4. Listen and say which room or place the people are in
1. In the ....
2. In the ....
3. In the ....
4. In the ....
5. In the ....
6. In the ....
7. In the ....

5. Draw a plan of your house or flat. Tell your partner about the rooms

 Set 2   **Express satisfaction and dissatisfaction**

Mmm! It's nice and big!

1. Look at this advertisement for a holiday in Spain

Mr and Mrs Ferm go and stay at the Hotel Casa Blanca. They are very satisfied with the holiday. Look at the photographs from their holiday and write what they say

Oh! It isn't very big.

3. **Mr and Mrs Case go and stay at another hotel, the Hotel Casa Brava. They aren't very satisfied with the holiday. Look at the photographs from their holiday and write what they say.** (For picture 1. Mrs Case says: 'Oh! It isn't very comfortable.')

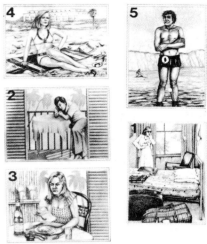

4. **Now show your partner the holiday photographs again. This time sound dissatisfied!**

5. **Look at your plan of your house or flat. Tell your partner again about the rooms and about the size, like this:**

➡ This is the bathroom.
It's nice and big.
or
It isn't very big.

6. **Now say something about these things:**

> *your town*
> *your flat or house*
> *your classroom*
> *the weather*
> *English food*

Use these words: big/comfortable/clean/tasty/warm/:

➡ It's nice and ....
or
It isn't very ....

7. **Collect your own holiday photographs, and show them to your partner or your group.**

2. **Now work with a partner. You go on holiday too. Show each other the holiday photographs, like this:**

➡ Here's the hotel ....
Mmm! It's nice and ....
Try to sound satisfied!

MRS PARKER:	Well, that's the flat. Come and have a cup of tea.
JACKIE:	Oh, thank you very much.
MRS PARKER:	Are you English?
JACKIE:	No, I'm not. I'm Australian. I'm from Melbourne but I live in Trafford now.
MRS PARKER:	I see. Are you married?
JACKIE:	No, I'm not. Er… how much it? The flat, I mean.
MRS PARKER:	It's £14 a week.
JACKIE:	£14… Mmm… Can I telephone you tomorrow?
MRS PARKER:	Yes, of course. My number is 334 8956.
JACKIE:	334 8946.
MRS PARKER:	No, 8956.
JACKIE:	I'm sorry – 334 8956. Right! Well, goodbye and thank you for the tea.
MRS PARKER:	Goodbye!
JACKIE:	Goodbye!

Set 3   Ask and talk about cost.

How much is it? It's £14.

10	ten
11	eleven
12	twelve
13	thirteen
14	fourteen
15	fifteen
16	sixteen
17	seventeen
18	eighteen
19	nineteen
20	twenty
£1	= one pound
£14	= fourteen pounds

1. Read these prices and write them down in words.

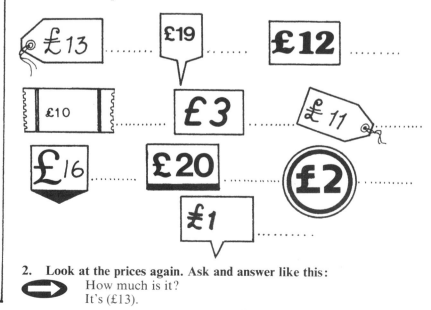

2. Look at the prices again. Ask and answer like this:

➡ How much is it?
It's (£13).

EXTENSION

1. This house is for sale. It's in Brighton.

Houses For Sale

BRIGHTON: comfortable family house near shops and station. 3 beds, 1 sit. room, 1 din.room, kit, bathroom and toilet, garage and small garden. £25,000. Tel: Brighton 44788 Mrs Kite

Here is a list of rooms and extras in this Brighton house:

3 bedrooms	a kitchen	a garage
a sitting room	a bathroom	a garden
a dining room	a toilet	

Make a list of rooms in your house or flat

2. Martin and Cathy Ford buy the house in Brighton. This is the letter they send to a friend of theirs, Lucy:

Miss Lucy Simpson,
19, Cartland Road,
LONDON, S.W.8.

17, Sherman Road,
Brighton,
Sussex.
18.10.7..

Dear Lucy,
        This is the new address of our house. The house is nice and big — 3 bedrooms, a sitting room, a dining room, kitchen, bathroom and toilet. Oh yes, _and_ a garden! The garden isn't very big but it's fine for us. The house is near the station so come and see us soon.
                Love,
                Cathy and Martin.

UNIT 9

3. You move into a new flat or house. Write a letter to a friend and tell him or her about the new flat or house. Write the envelope to your friend too.

4. Listen to the tape and write down the rooms and places Tessa and David see, in order

1. The hall
2. ....
3. ....
4. ....
5. ....
6. ....
7. ....
8. ....

An English House

Many English houses have two floors, an upstairs and a downstairs. The bedrooms, the bathroom and the toilet are usually upstairs, and the sitting room, the kitchen and dining-room are downstairs. There is usually a small garden at the back of the house. Some people who live alone sometimes let the upstairs of the house and make it into a small flat.

OPEN DIALOGUE

Talk to Tessa. Show her your flat or house. Show her the sitting room, the bedroom, the kitchen and the bathroom.

TESSA: Hello!
STUDENT: ....
TESSA: Is this your new flat?
STUDENT: ....
TESSA: Do show me round. What's this room?
STUDENT: ....
TESSA: Oh, yes, it's nice and big.
STUDENT: ....
TESSA: Mmm! It looks very comfortable. Is this the kitchen?
STUDENT: ....
TESSA: It's very nice. And what's this room?
STUDENT: ....
TESSA: Oh yes. Well, it's lovely. Thank you. Goodbye!
STUDENT: ....

ORAL EXERCISES

1. Show where rooms are (1)
Can you show me the sitting room?
Yes, this is the sitting room.

Can you show me the kitchen?
Yes, this is the kitchen.

2. Show where rooms are (2)
Is this the sitting room?
No, it isn't. That's the sitting room over there.

Is this the kitchen?
No, it isn't. That's the kitchen over there.

3. Ask about the rooms
You want to find the bedroom.
Is this the bedroom?

You want to find the bathroom.
Is this the bathroom?

4. Ask about prices. Look at page 50
How much is it? 13?
Yes, that's right. It's £13.

How much is it? £19?
Yes, that's right. It's £19.

5. You are on holiday. Express satisfaction about things
Is your hotel room big?
Yes, it's nice and big.

And is it clean?
Yes, it's nice and clean.

6. You are still on holiday. This time express dissatisfaction
Is your hotel room big?
No, it isn't very big.

And clean, I suppose.
No, it isn't very clean.

REMEMBER

This is how you:

1.	Show and ask about places	This is the kitchen. Is this the kitchen? Yes, it is./No, it isn't.
2.	Express satisfaction	Mmm! It's nice and big.
3.	Express dissatisfaction	Oh! It isn't very big.
4.	Ask and talk about cost	How much is it? It's £14.

Grammar

This is That's	the	bedroom bathroom kitchen

Is	this that	the	bedroom bathroom? kitchen

Yes, it is
No, it isn't

It's nice and	big hot cold

It isn't very	big hot cold

How much is it?

It's	£13 £1 £20	a week

Words and Phrases

a house	a pound	very	ten	upstairs	show
a sitting room	a week	big	eleven	downstairs	
a bathroom		hot	twelve		
a kitchen	food	cold	thirteen	Dear . . .	
a toilet	temperature	warm	fourteen	Love . . .	
a dining room		comfortable	fifteen		
a hall		clean	sixteen		
a garage		tasty	seventeen		
a garden			eighteen		
a terrace		how much?	nineteen		
a beach			twenty		

the sea
the weather

a classroom

Coffee Time

UNIT 10

NEVILLE: **Jackie! It's coffee time!**
JACKIE: **Coming!**
NEVILLE: **Well, this is the cafeteria.**
JACKIE: **It's nice and modern!**
NEVILLE: **Would you like a cup of coffee?**
JACKIE: **Yes, please.**
NEVILLE: **And a biscuit?**
JACKIE: **No, thanks. Just a cup of coffee.**

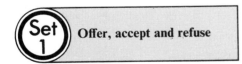

Set 1   **Offer, accept and refuse**

Would you like a cup of coffee?	Yes, please.
And a biscuit?	No, thanks.

1. **Look at the picture and offer things to eat and drink, like this:**
   ➡️   Would you like a cup of coffee?
        Would you like a ....?

2. **Accept the things your partner offers, like this:**
   ➡️   Would you like a cup of coffee?
        Yes, please.

        Would you like a glass of beer?
        ....

        Would you like a sandwich?
        ....

a glass of w
a cup of tea
a glass o
a cup of coffee
a glass c
a cake
a biscuit
a glass of beer   a sandw

3. Now refuse the things your partner offers, like this:

Would you like a cup of coffee?
No, thanks.

Would you like a glass of beer?
....

4. Offer your partner something to drink first, and then something to to eat, like this:

Would you like a cup of coffee?
Yes, please.
And a biscuit?
No, thanks. Just a cup of coffee.

---

a cup of tea/a biscuit   a glass of beer/a sandwich
a glass of milk/a cake   a cup of coffee/a biscuit
a glass of wine/a sandwich

NEVILLE: **Good morning, Mrs Jenkins. Can I have a cup of coffee please – no, can I have two cups of coffee, please?**

MRS JENKINS: **Two cups of coffee. Yes, here you are. That's 24 pence.**

NEVILLE: **24 pence. Here you are.**

MRS J: **Thank you.**

NEVILLE: **Here's your coffee, Jackie. It's white. Is that all right?**

JACKIE: **Oh yes, that's fine, thanks. How much is it?**

NEVILLE: **It's 12p. But I'll pay.**

JACKIE: **Oh, thank you very much. Mmm! It's nice and strong.**

> *Good morning, Mrs. Jenkins. Can I have a cup of coffee please – no, can I have two cups of coffee, please?*

> *Two cups of coffee. Yes, here you are. That's 24 pence.*

Set 2 **Ask people for things
Give people things**

Can I have a cup of coffee, please? Yes, here you are.

---

1. Look at the pictures on page 54. Ask for and give the things in the pictures, like this:

Can I have a cup of coffee, please?
Yes, here you are.

Can I have ....?
Yes, here you are.

Can I have two cups of coffee, please? Yes, here you are.

---

one cup — two cup*s*
one biscuit — two biscuits
one cake — two cakes

one glass — two glass*es*
one sandwich — two sandwiches

2. Now ask for TWO of everything in the pictures, like this:

Can I have two cups of coffee, please?
Two cups of coffee. Yes, here you are.

Can I have two ...., please?
Two .... Yes, here you are.

3. Look again at the pictures of things to eat and drink, and offer your partner something to eat and drink. When your partner accepts, ask for two of the same thing: one for your partner and one for yourself. Here is an example:

Would you like a sandwich?
Yes, please.
Can I have two sandwiches, please?

(Set 3) **Ask and talk about cost**

Numbers 20-100

20 twenty   **21** twenty one
22 twenty two   **23** twenty three
30 thirty   **40** forty   **50** fifty
60 sixty   **70** seventy **80** eighty
90 ninety   **100** a hundred

35p = thirty-five pence (or p.)
£1.35 = one pound thirty-five (pence)
£2.35 = two pounds thirty-five (pence)
£2.00 = two pounds

(i) **59p**   (ii) **86p**   (iii) **£3.45**
(iv) **£1.99**   (v) **£27.00**
(vi) **£100.00**   (vii) **£2.75**

1. Read these prices

Focus Cafeteria

PRICE LIST

DRINKS

Coffee	12p
Tea	10p
Milk	10p
Orange Juice	12p
Chocolate	15p
Coca Cola	12p

SNACKS

Cakes	10p each
Biscuits (per packet)	8p
Sandwiches	22p each

How much is a cup of coffee? It's 12p.

2. Ask and answer about the prices, like this:

➡ How much is a cup of coffee and a cup of tea?
How much is a cup of tea and a glass of milk?
How much is a cup of chocolate and a packet of biscuits?

Ask 5 more questions about the prices.

3. Group work.
Get into groups of three or four. Look at the menu and say what you want to eat and drink, like this:

➡ A sandwich and a cup of tea, please.
A ...., please.

Make a list of what everyone in the group wants, like this:

2 sandwiches
3 cakes
2 cups of tea
1 cup of coffee
1 orange juice
1 packet of biscuits

How much is it altogether? Work it out.

EXTENSION

Listen to the tape and fill in these sentences

Peter is from ....
He's an ....
Murray offers Tessa and Peter a ....
Tessa wants ....
Peter wants ....
Murray wants ....
Murray orders two .... and a ....
It costs ....

UNIT 10

OPEN DIALOGUE

Neville and his friend, Maria, meet you in a cafeteria.

NEVILLE: Oh, hello!

STUDENT: ....

NEVILLE: Meet Maria. Maria's a student too.

STUDENT: ....

MARIA: Hello.

NEVILLE: Listen, I must go now. It's late. I'll see you later Maria.
Goodbye, you two.

STUDENT: ....

MARIA: What's your name, by the way? Your first name.

STUDENT: ....

MARIA: Sorry, what?

STUDENT: ....

MARIA: Oh... are you English?

STUDENT: ....

MARIA: Oh, are you? Well, would you like a cup of coffee?

STUDENT: ....

MARIA: And a biscuit?

STUDENT: ....

MARIA: Right. And don't worry – I'll pay.

STUDENT: ....

ORAL EXERCISES

1. Offer people something to eat or drink
Ah, here's Murray! Offer him a cup of
coffee.
Would you like a cup of coffee, Murray?

Ah, here's Tessa! Offer her a cup of tea.
Would you like a cup of tea, Tessa?

2. Ask for something to eat or drink
A cup of tea or a cup of coffee?
Can I have a cup of coffee, please.

A glass of milk or a glass of water?
Can I have a glass of water, please.

3. Ask again – this time for yourself and a friend
I think I'd like a cup of tea.
Right! Can I have two cups of tea, please.

I think I'd like a glass of milk.
Right! Can I have two glasses of milk, please.

4. Ask the price of things
I think I'll have a cup of coffee.
How much is it?

I think I'll get some cakes.
How much are they?

5. Say how much things cost. Look at page 57
How much is a coffee?
It's 12 pence.

How much are the sandwiches?
They're 22 pence each.

6. A Rhyme
Tea for me
Coffee for you
Coffee and tea
For you and me
Coffee, tea and biscuits
Coffee, tea and biscuits
Coffee, tea and biscuits
And a cake for you and me.

```
Memorandum
_____

To   All employees at Focus Films
          FROM:  Peter Bates, Personnel Manager


Date   7th October
_____

Subject   i)  The Canteen Manageress
          ii) Canteen Prices

   i)  I am sorry to say that Mrs Jenkins, our canteen
       manageress, is ill in hospital. As you know, the
       cafeteria is very busy between 11 and 2 o'clock.
       We would like some extra help while Mrs Jenkins
       is away.  If you can help any day next week,  can
       I have your name before Friday, October 9th.

   ii) From Monday. October 12th, coffee and sandwiches
       will cost 2p extra, and all other items on the
       cafeteria menu 1p extra.

                    Signed:  Peter Bates

                             Peter Bates,
                             Personnel Manager.
```

REMEMBER

This is how you:
1. Offer something   Would you like a cup of tea?
   Accept something   Yes please.
   Refuse something   No thanks.
2. Ask for and give things   Can I have a biscuit please.
                        Yes, here you are.

Grammar

Would you like a	cup of tea coffee? glass of milk biscuit

Can I have a	cup of tea coffee glass of milk biscuit

one cup – two cups one glass – two glasses one sandwich – two sandwiches

Words and Phrases

a cup	coffee	red	yes, please	twenty-one	pay
a glass	tea	white	no, thanks	twenty-two	speak
a packet	water	strong	can I have . . .	twenty-three	
a cafeteria	milk	modern	just	thirty	
a biscuit	wine		here you are	forty	
a cake	beer	each	right	fifty	
a sandwich	orange juice		Bye!	sixty	
	chocolate		don't worry	seventy	
	pence			eighty	
	money			ninety	
				a hundred	

Do you like tea with lemon?

UNIT 11

IN MARIA'S FLAT

What's the time Maria?

It's four o'clock. Would you like a cup of tea?

Mmm! Yes, please.

NEVILLE:	What's the time, Maria?
MARIA:	It's four o'clock. Would you like a cup of tea?
NEVILLE:	Mmm! Yes, please.
MARIA:	Do you like tea with lemon?
NEVILLE:	Yes, I do.
MARIA:	Oh good. Here you are .... Sugar?
NEVILLE:	Yes please.
MARIA:	Mind the cup!
NEVILLE:	Oh, sorry!
MARIA:	That's all right! I'll get a cloth. Let's have some music. Do you like Rita Hamilton?
NEVILLE:	Yes, she's all right.
MARIA:	Well, *I* like her. I think she's very good.

Set 1 — Ask and say the time (1)

What's the time?   It's four o'clock.

1

four o'clock

3

half past four

2

quarter past four

4

quarter to five

1 2 3 4 5

6 7 8 9 10

11

12

1. Look at these clocks. Ask and answer like this:

⟹
1. What's the time?
    It's three o'clock.

2. What's the time?
    It's half past four.

3. What's the time?
    It's ....

Is it three o'clock? Yes, it is.

2. Look at the clocks again. Ask and answer like this:

➡ 1. Is it three o'clock?
   Yes, it is.
2. Is it ....?
   Yes, it is.

**(Set 2) Ask what people like
Say what you like**

Do you like tea with lemon? Yes, I do.
Do you like sightseeing? No, I don't.

Do you like Frank Sinatra?	He's all right.
Do you like Elizabeth Taylor?	She's all right.
Do you like the Rolling Stones?	They're all right.
Do you like small dogs?	They're all right.
Do you like classical music?	It's all right.
Do you like whisky?	It's all right.

DO YOU LIKE:	YOU	YOUR PARTNER	DO YOU LIKE:	YOU	YOUR PARTNER
Tea with lemon			Small dogs		
Tea with milk			American films		
White coffee			Detective stories		
Black coffee			Spiders		
Coca-cola			Jazz		
Whisky			Classical music		
Sightseeing					
Sunbathing					
Writing letters					
Cooking					

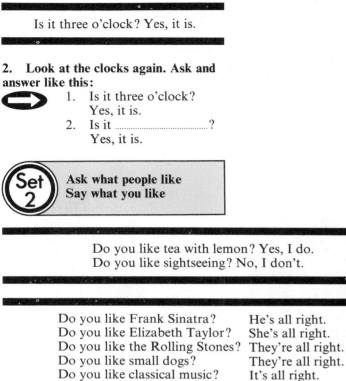

1. Look at the chart. Write in your answers:
Yes/No/AR (it's all right – you like it but not very much)

2. Now ask your partner what he/she likes, like this:

Do you like tea with lemon?
Yes I do/No I don't/It's all right.

Write in his/her answer also: (Yes/No/AR)

> **When you answer about the people, remember to say:**
> *He's/She's/They're* all right
>
> **and when you answer about more than one thing, you say:** *They're* all right

 Ask and say what people like

Does he like tea with milk?	Yes, he does.
black coffee?	No, he doesn't.
coca–cola?	He thinks it's all right.

Does she like jazz?	Yes, she does.
classical music?	No, she doesn't.
Frank Sinatra?	She thinks he's all right.

<u>Yes</u>.	<u>No</u>.	<u>All right</u>.
white coffee	black coffee	sunbathing
tea with lemon	coca-cola	whisky
detective stories	Frank Sinatra	cooking
Elizabeth Taylor	small dogs	pop-music
jazz	sightseeing	the Rolling Stones
spiders	writing letters	detective stories

1. Look at Neville's answers to the questions. Work with a partner.
Ask and answer like this:

Does he like tea with lemon?
Yes he does.

Does he like black coffee?
No he doesn't.

Does he like sunbathing?
He thinks it's all right.

First ask about the 'Yes list, then the 'No' list and then the 'All right' list.

<u>Yes.</u>	<u>No.</u>	<u>All right.</u>
black coffee	white coffee	writing letters
sunbathing	whisky	coca-cola
cooking	Frank Sinatra	sightseeing
American films	jazz	Elizabeth Taylor
small dogs	spiders	detective stories
tea with lemon	tea with milk	

**2. Look at Maria's answers to the questions. Work with a partner.
Ask and answer like this:**

     Does she like black coffee?
Yes she does.

Does she like spiders?
No she doesn't.

Does she like coca-cola?
She thinks it's all right.

Work as in Exercise 1

**3. Look at your partner's answers to the questions on page 61.
Work with a new partner (somebody else in the class). Ask and answer
about your *first* partner's answers, like this:**

     Does he/she like tea with lemon?
Yes, he/she does
    or
No, he/she doesn't
    or
He/she thinks it's all right.

4. Ask your teacher what he/she likes. Write in the answers

Does your teacher like white coffee? ....

              coca-cola? ....

              whisky? ....

              jazz? ....

              Frank Sinatra? ....

              spiders? ....

              cooking? ....

EXTENSION

1. **Jobs Vacant**

```
        BOUTIQUE ASSISTANT
Do you like PEOPLE ?
Do you like CLOTHES ?
Do you speak ENGLISH, FRENCH
& GERMAN ?
Are you between 20 and 30 ?
If your answer is 'YES' to
these questions...........
Write to Ms Marianne Weston
at the EUROBOUTIQUE,
Manchester International
Airport, Manchester.
```

Mother's Help or Au-pair girl wanted for:
Mark, 5, and Wendy, 2½

Are you over 18?
Do you like CHILDREN?
Do you like COOKING?
Do you want to learn ENGLISH?
Can you DRIVE?

If so, please write and give
full particulars to:
Mrs. Trafford,
8, Talbot Square,
London, W.8.

DRIVER WANTED
TO TEST-DRIVE
OUR NEW MODELS

IF YOU LIKE <u>CARS</u>
IF YOU CAN <u>DRIVE</u>
AND <u>IF</u> YOU'RE OVER 21

WRITE TO THE MANAGER:-

DALTON MOTORS·KINGSTON·SURREY

**Choose one of the three jobs advertised and write a letter
applying for the job. Start like this:**

Dear ....
        My name is .... and I'm ( ) years old.

Then write sentences starting like this:

I like ....
I speak ....
I can ....
I want to ....

Finish your letter like this:

If you would like to telephone me, my number is ....
                Yours faithfully,

                (SIGNATURE)

2.

Name: Michèle Boileau		Yes	No	A/R
Does she	like children?			
	cooking?			
	speak English?			
Can she drive?				
Does she smoke?				
Does she like	music?			
	classical music?			
	jazz?			
	reading?			
Other interest..........................				
Does she get the job?				

OPEN DIALOGUE

You go to see Neville in his flat

NEVILLE: Hello.
STUDENT: ....
NEVILLE: Come in, please.
STUDENT: ....
NEVILLE: What's the time? My watch is wrong, I think.
STUDENT: ....
NEVILLE: Thank you. Well, would you like a cup of coffee?
STUDENT: ....
NEVILLE: Do you like white coffee?
STUDENT: ....
NEVILLE: Sugar?
STUDENT: ....
NEVILLE: Right. Just one moment... Here you are.
STUDENT: ....
NEVILLE: Mind the cup!
STUDENT: ....
NEVILLE: Oh, that's all right. I'll get a cloth. Let's have some music. Do you like pop music?
STUDENT: ....
NEVILLE: Oh, one moment. Here's an Eagles record. Do you like the Eagles?
STUDENT: ....
NEVILLE: Well, I think they're very good.

ORAL EXERCISES

1. Say the correct time. Look at the clocks on page 60

Is it three o'clock?
Yes, it is.

Is it half past five?
No, it isn't, it's half past four.

2. Ask Neville what he likes

Ask him if he likes tea with lemon.
Do you like tea with lemon?

Ask him if he likes black coffee.
Do you like black coffee?

3. Say what you like or don't like. You are Neville. Look at the chart on page 62.

Do you like tea with lemon?
Yes, I do.

Do you like black coffee?
No, I don't.

Do you like whisky?
It's all right.

4. Ask what other people like.

Ask if Maria likes sightseeing.
Does she like sightseeing?

Ask if Neville likes spiders.
Does he like spiders?

5. Say what Maria likes or doesn't like. Look at her chart on page 63.

Does she like sunbathing?
Yes, she does.

Does she like white coffee?
No, she doesn't.

Does she like writing letters?
She thinks it's all right.

6. Say what you like/or don't like

Do you like sightseeing?

....

Do you like small dogs?

....

UNIT 11

A Focus Survey

by Sally Baker

Focus Films, a documentary film company here in Manchester, is making a film to show in schools. The film is about teenagers and their parents, what they like and what they don't like.

The film shows that they do not always like the same things. Some of the answers are amusing, but some are worrying.

Murray Freeman, the director of the film, asks questions like: 'Do you like the government?' Here are some typical answers: Terry, aged 16 says he doesn't, his father says it's all right, and his mother says she thinks it's a very good government!

Murray also asks: 'Do you like watching television?' More than 80% of the parents say 'Yes, we do', but more than 50% of the teenagers say 'No, we don't'.

One other question is: 'Do you like talking to your parents/children?. And the answer? 'Talking? What do you mean?'

The film is interesting and worrying. All teenagers *and* parents should see it.

REMEMBER

This is how you:

1.	Ask the time	What's the time?
2.	Say the time	It's two o'clock.
		It's half past two.
		It's quarter to/past two.
3.	Ask what people like	Do you like tea with lemon?
		Does he like tea with lemon?
4.	Say what you like	Yes I do./No I don't.
		It's all right.
5.	Say what other people like	Yes he does./No, he doesn't.
		He thinks it's all right.
6.	Apologise	Sorry!
7.	Accept apologies	That's all right!

Grammar

Do	you				Yes	I	do		No	I	don't
Does	he she	like	tea with lemon?			he she	does			he she	doesn't

He She	thinks	it's he's she's they're	all right

Words and Phrases

a dog	sugar	sightsee(ing)	like	all right (he's . . .)	what's the time?
a spider	lemon	sunbathe	think	sorry!	o'clock (one o'clock)
a detective story	whisky	(sunbathing)	drive	that's all right!	past (quarter past)
a record	coca-cola	cook(ing)	smoke	with	to (quarter to)
a letter	classical music	read(ing)	want	(tea with milk)	quarter
a watch	jazz	write	learn	black	half
children		(writing)	speak	(black coffee)	
(a child)			get	wrong	
clothes			ask		
			answer		

UNIT 12

Consolidation Unit

At the Manchester International Club

PART 1.

MARIA: **Excuse me!**

MAN: **Yes?**

MARIA: **Where's the International Club?**

MAN: **It's over there, next to the cinema.**

MARIA: **Oh yes. Thank you.**

PART 2.

GIRL: **Name please.**

MARIA: **Maria Magnani.**

GIRL: **Are you a member?**

MARIA: **No, I'm not.**

GIRL: **Oh, well, it's 50p please.**

MARIA: **Sorry, how much is it?**

GIRL: **50p... 50 pence.**

MARIA: **Oh, I see... here you are... Where's the cloakroom?**

GIRL: **It's here. This is the cloakroom, and that's the clubroom in there.**

MARIA: **Thank you.**

PART 3

JOE: **Hello! I'm Joe. What's your name?**

MARIA: **Maria.**

JOE: **Oh, are you English?**

MARIA: **No, I'm not. I'm Italian. And you?**

JOE: **I'm American.**

MARIA: **Oh. Do you speak Italian?**

JOE: **No, I don't. Sorry!**

MARIA: **Oh, that's all right.**

PART 4

JOE: **Would you like a drink, Maria?**

MARIA: **Yes, please.**

JOE: **Beer, wine or coca-cola?**

MARIA: **Wine please. White wine.**

JOE: **Can I have two glasses of white wine, please.**

MARIA: **Oh, thanks.**

JOE: **Cheers!**

MARIA: **Cheers!**

JOE: **Oh, it isn't very good.**

MARIA: **No, but it's nice and cold.**

PART 5

JOE: **Do you like Manchester, Maria?**

MARIA: **It's all right.**

JOE: **Where are you from in Italy?**

MARIA: **From the north. From Milan. Where are you from?**

JOE: **I'm from California. But I live in Manchester now, well, a suburb of Manchester. I'm a student at the University.**

PART 6

JOE: **Oh, this is a Breakaway record. Do you like Breakaway?**

MARIA: **Yes, I do. They're very good. Well, would you like a dance?**

JOE: **Yes, all right.**

PART 7

MARIA: **What's the time?**

JOE: **It's quarter past eleven.**

MARIA: **Oh, I must go.**

JOE: **Oh... what's your telephone number?**

MARIA: **It's 477 9372.**

JOE: **4.7.7....9.3.7.2. Right! Well, can I telephone you soon? Is that all right?**

MARIA: **Yes, that's fine. Well, bye!... and thanks for a lovely evening.**

JOE: **Bye!**

1. Read the dialogue with your partner. One of you can be Maria, the other can be the man in part 1, the girl in part 2, and Joe in parts 3–7.

UNIT 12

2. Read parts 3, 4, 5 and 7 again with your partner. This time say your own name and nationality; say what you would like to drink; say where you are from and where you live now; and say your own telephone number. Change parts afterwards.

3. **Fill in the missing words in the gaps. Choose from these words:**

am   'm not   do   don't
is   isn't   does   doesn't
are   aren't
         's

1. Where _____ you live?
2. What _____ he do?
3. _____ you like tea?
No, I _____
4. _____ you English?
No, I _____
5. Where _____ Mr and Mrs Brown live?
6. _____ they from Manchester? Yes, they _____
7. _____ you from London? Yes, I _____
8. What _____ you do?
9. _____ he Australian? No, he _____
10. _____ he like jazz? No, he _____
11. _____ she like Mozart? Yes, she _____
12. _____ you from London? No, we _____
13. What _____ she do? She _____ a journalist.

4. **Allan Simmons goes to see Maria in her flat. Write in what Maria says**

MARIA: Come in, Allan _____
ALLAN: Mmm! It's nice and big. My flat is very small.
MARIA: _____
ALLAN: Yes, please. But no milk. I like black coffee.
MARIA: _____
ALLAN: Thank you. Mmm! It's nice and strong.
MARIA: _____
ALLAN: I live in a suburb south of Manchester. Where are you from, Maria?
MARIA: _____
ALLAN: Milan! That's nice.
MARIA: _____
ALLAN: Manchester? Yes, I do. I like big towns. Do you like it here?
MARIA: _____
ALLAN: Well, I must go soon. It's late.
MARIA: _____
ALLAN: It's half past four. I must telephone Focus Films. Where's the telephone?
MARIA: _____
ALLAN: Oh, where's the bedroom? Is this the bedroom?
MARIA: _____
ALLAN: Right – thanks.

Now read the dialogue with your partner

5. **A letter from Maria to an English friend**

> 14 Sutton Road
> Manchester
> 12th February
>
> Dear Ann,
>   Thank you for your long letter. I'm not a good letter writer --- sorry!
>   Yes, I'm now in Manchester. I live in a flat near the centre with four Italian girls. They're all right but they speak Italian all the time! The flat isn't very big so I sleep in the sitting-room.
>   You ask if I like Manchester. Yes, it's all right but it's a big town and it's a little lonely sometimes. I know one or two people now – Neville and Joe for example. Neville works for a film company. I met Joe at the International Club here. He's American, from California. He's a student here at the University. He's very nice but he speaks very quickly!
>   The English lessons are all right but we are 25 in our class. But the teacher is very good. My English is a little better I think.
>   Well, it's quarter to twelve and I'm very tired. Sorry this letter is so short. Please write again soon.
>   Love from   Maria

6. **Fill in the right responses using these adjectives**

my   her
your   our
his   their

e.g. Is that John's car? No, that's his car over there.

1. Is that Tessa's house? ....

2. Is that Murray's car? ....

3. Is that your car? ....

4. Is that the Freemans' house? ....

5. Is that my room? ....

6. Is that Tessa's and my office? ....

7. Is that Jackie's coffee? ....

8. Is that our bus, Allan? ....

7. A Food and Drink Crossword

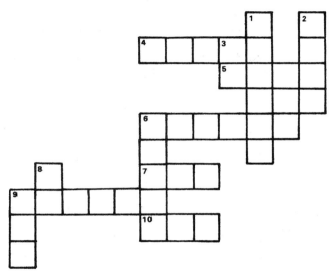

Clues

Across   4. Coffee? Yes, please. With ....? No, thanks, just milk.   **5.** A glass of ...., please. **6.** A strong drink.   **7.** English people drink this at four o'clock.   **9.** This .... is nice and strong.   **10.** .... wine or white wine?

Down   1. Tea, orange-juice and coca-cola are .... **2.** Do you .... tea with lemon? **3.** I .... English, not American. **6.** Would you like a glass of beer or wine? No thanks. Just .... please.   **8.** .... you like coca-cola? Yes, I .... **9.** Would you like a .... of coffee?

REMEMBER
Words and Phrases

a drink	good	soon	sleep
a university	lonely	quickly	dance
a lesson	short	again	
a class	little		
a town	Italian	cheers!	
a place			
a club			

Train to Coventry

Murray, Neville and Jackie go to Coventry to do a film.

MURRAY: **Three to Coventry, please.**
MAN: **Single or return?**
MURRAY: **Return please.**
NEVILLE: **Hurry up, Murray! It's late. It's ten past nine!**

Set 1   Ask and say the time (2)

What's the time? It's ten past nine.

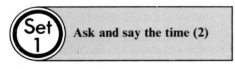

| five past nine | ten past nine | twenty past nine | twenty five past nine | twenty five to ten | twenty to ten | ten to ten | five to ten |

1. Ask and answer like this:

1. What's the time?
   It's five past two.

2. What's the time?
   It's twenty past four.

2. Say these times and write them

13.25 twenty-five past one	16.55 ....
8.05	5.10 ....
21.35	18.40 ....
19.20	11.35 ....
2.50	22.50 ....

MURRAY: **What time does the train leave?**

JACKIE: **It leaves at twenty-past nine.**

MURRAY: **Which platform does it leave from?**

JACKIE: **Platform Nine. It's over there.**

MURRAY: **All right, let's go!**

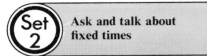

Ask and talk about fixed times

	LEAVE	ARRIVE		START	FINISH	OPEN	CLOSE
BUS	11·05	11·20	**FILM**	7·15	9·00		
TRAIN	9·20	9·40	**MATCH**	3·00	4·45		
PLANE	1·15	3·50	**BANK**			9·30	3·30
			POST OFFICE			9·00	5·30

What time does the train leave?
It leaves at twenty past nine.

1. Ask and answer like this:

What time does the bus leave?
It leaves at five past eleven.

What time does it arrive?
It arrives at twenty past eleven.

What time does the train leave?

....

What time does it arrive?

....

2. Write notes to people like this:

The bus leaves at 11·05 and arrives at 11·20. Meet me at 11·20.

Meet me at . . .

The train leaves at ....

The plane ....

The film starts at ....

The match ....

The bank closes at ....

The post office ....

a.m. = morning
p.m. = afternoon   (1 p.m.–6 p.m.)
       evening   (6 p.m.–12 a.m.)

3 a.m. = three o'clock in the morning
3 p.m. = three o'clock in the afternoon
8 p.m. = eight o'clock in the evening

3. Say all the times in a different way. Look at the example in sentence 1

1. The train leaves at 6 a.m.
   The train leaves at six o'clock in the morning.
2. The bus leaves at 7 p.m.
   The bus leaves at ....
3. The plane arrives at 1.30 a.m.
   ....
4. The film starts at 9 p.m.
   ....
5. The film finishes at 10.45 p.m.
   ....
6. The bank closes at 3.30 p.m.
   ....

4. Look at the information. Ask and answer like this:

What time does the shop open? It opens at 9 o'clock.
What time does the shop close? ....

GATE CINEMA Nott Hill 727 5750
Wenders **KINGS OF THE ROAD**
(AA) 1.30, 4.35, 8.00. **THE CON-**
FORMIST (X) & MURDER
CZECH STYLE (X) 11.15
JACEY LEICESTER SQUARE (437
2001). **BLACK EMMANUELLE**
WHITE EMMANUELLE (X) plus
CAGED WOMEN (X). Progs 3.30,
5.00, 7.40.
LEICESTER SQUARE THEATRE
(930 5252). **NETWORK (AA).** Sep.
progs Today. 2.00, 5.15, 8.26. Seats
bkble for 8.25 prog Mon-Fri & all
progs Sat & Sun except late night
show.
LONDON PAVILION. Picc Circus
(437 2982). **CARRIE (X)** Cont progs
Today 3.55, 6.10, 8.25.
ODEON HAYMARKET (930 2738/
2771) Mel Brooks **SILENT MOVIE**
(A) Sep. progs. Today 5.30, 8.30.

EXTENSION

MANCHESTER INTERNATIONAL AIRPORT
Domestic Passenger Arrivals

	Airline	Flight No.	Day	Dep	Arr
Birmingham	DA	DA053	Daily	0900	0935
Bristol	DA	DA055	Daily	1845	2005
Edinburgh	BE	BE916	Daily	0840	0925
Edinburgh	BE	BE4483	Daily	1835	1920
London	BE	BE4406	Daily	0800	0845
London	BE	BE4424	Daily	1415	1500
Newcastle	DA	DA052	Daily	0750	0835
Newcastle	DA	DA056	Daily	1800	1845

1. Roleplay
You go into a travel agency in Manchester. You want to be in London at 10 a.m. Work with a partner. Find out:
- *a)* What time your plane leaves Manchester
- *b)* What time it arrives at London airport
- *c)* What your flight number is

Now do the same for these situations:
> You want to be in Edinburgh at 8 p.m.
> You want to be in Birmingham at 10.30 a.m.
> You want to be in Newcastle at 9 a.m.

```
Tourist Information Board          July 14th-21st


WELCOME TO SLAXTON-ON-SEA
*************************


Here is some practical information about the town to
help you make your stay as pleasant and enjoyable as
possible.


BANKS

Lloyds     44 High St.    Hours 9.30 a.m. - 3.30 p.m.
                          (Thursday also
                                   4.30 - 6.00 p.m.)

Barclays   31 High St.    Hours 9.30 a.m. - 3.30 p.m.

National Westminster
           14 George St. Hours 9.30 a.m. - 3.30 p.m.


POST OFFICE

           51 High St.    Hours 9.00 a.m. - 5.30 p.m.
```

```
DEPARTMENT STORES

Whitings    12 West St.    Hours 9.00 a.m. - 6.00 p.m.
                           Late night Monday 9.00 a.m.
                                            - 7.00 p.m.
                           Early closing Thursday
                                            1.00 p.m.

John Manns 46 High St.    Hours 9.00 a.m. - 6.00 p.m.
                           Early closing Thursday
                                            1.00 p.m.

CINEMAS

The Odeon   High St.    Showing this week July 14 - 21
                        "Holiday Fun" Perf 7.00 - 8.45

The Rex     George St.  Showing this week until
                                            Wednesday
                        "A Day in the Life"
                                    Perf 7.15 - 9.00
                        From Wednesday
                        "Flight to Hong Kong"
                                    Perf 7.00 - 8.45

ENJOY YOUR STAY IN SLAXTON-ON-SEA
*********************************
```

2.
Find out the same information for your town. Write the information for your brochure.

UNIT 13

3. 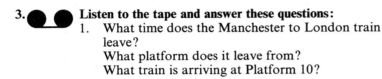 **Listen to the tape and answer these questions:**
1. What time does the Manchester to London train leave?
   What platform does it leave from?
   What train is arriving at Platform 10?

2. What is the flight number?
   What time is the flight leaving now?

OPEN DIALOGUE

Look at the flight timetable on page 73. You want to go to London tomorrow. Choose a flight and write down the times and the flight number. Now talk to Allan.

ALLAN: Hello.
STUDENT: ....
ALLAN: You're going to London tomorrow, aren't you?
STUDENT: ....
ALLAN: What time does the flight leave Manchester?
STUDENT: ....
ALLAN: Is that in the morning or in the evening?
STUDENT: ....
ALLAN: Oh, well, I'll take you to the airport in my van.
STUDENT: ....
ALLAN: That's all right. What time does the flight arrive in London?
STUDENT: ....
ALLAN: Oh, that's nice and quick. Well, I'll see you tomorrow then. Goodbye for now!
STUDENT: ....

34 Maple Drive
Didsbury,
Manchester.
Oct 14th.

Dear Pat,
I must tell you about my new job. I work on the information desk at Manchester International airport.
I start at exactly half past eight in the morning, and the questions start at 8.31! Hundreds of people, hundreds of questions. 'What time does the plane for Milan leave?', 'What time does the flight from London arrive?', 'What time does the bank open?', 'What time does the bar close?', 'Where are the toilets?', 'Where are the taxis?'. The morning finishes at 12.30 and the questions start again at 1.30.
But I like it. I meet a lot of interesting people here — and I like the uniform too.
I must hurry — the post goes at half past five.
Lots of love,
Maureen

P.S Write soon!

ORAL EXERCISES

1. Ask what time things happen
The bus leaves soon. Hurry up!
What time does it leave?

The film starts soon. Hurry up!
What time does it start?

2. Say what time things happen. Look at the chart on page 71
What time does the bus arrive?
Let's see... it arrives at twenty past eleven.

What time does the film start?
Let's see... it starts at quarter past seven.

3. Ask exactly what time things happen
Talk to the travel agent
The plane arrives at five o'clock.
Five in the morning or five in the evening?

The bus leaves at one o'clock.
One in the morning or one in the afternoon?

4. Check the information
The train leaves at six hundred hours.
I see, it leaves at 6.00 a.m.

The bus leaves at nineteen hundred hours.
I see, it leaves at 7.00 p.m.

5. Correct the information politely
Look at the chart on page 71
I think the bus leaves at eleven o'clock.
No, it doesn't, it leaves at five past.

I think the train leaves at nine o'clock.
No, it doesn't, it leaves at twenty past.

REMEMBER

This is how you:

1. Ask the time	What's the time?
2. Say the time (minutes)	It's ten past three.
	It's five to four.
3. Ask what time things happen	What time does the train leave?
4. Say what time things happen	It leaves at five past nine.
	It arrives at six o'clock in the morning.

Grammar

What time does	the film it	start?	It	starts	at	7.15
	the bank it	open?		opens		ten past nine
	the bus it	arrive?		arrives		

It arrives at	4 o'clock	in the morning / afternoon
	8 o'clock	in the morning / evening

Words and Phrases

a train	a.m.	single	leave	hurry up!
a plane	p.m.	return	arrive	what time . . .
a flight	morning		start	(what time does it start?)
a match	afternoon	late	finish	let's see
a platform	evening		open	a lot of
a shop			close	
a film				

Shopping in Coventry

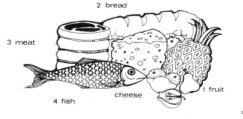

Well. Neville and I will pack up. Can you buy some fruit for the journey, Jack

Yes, of course.

At the factory, after filming.

MURRAY: Are we ready to go?

JACKIE: Yes, I think so.

SECRETARY: Focus Films? Yes, one moment. Mr Freeman, can you speak to Tessa Richards?

MURRAY: I'm sorry, I can't just now. We're in a hurry. It's late. The train leaves at ten past.

SECRETARY: All right. I'll tell her.

MURRAY: Thank you very much. Well, Neville and I will pack up. Can you buy some fruit for the journey, Jackie?

JACKIE: Yes, of course.

MURRAY: Can you meet us at the station afterwards?

JACKIE: Yes, O.K.

Set 1

Ask people to do things
Agree to do things
Say you can't do things

Can you buy some fruit?
Yes, of course.

1. Look at the pictures. Ask and answer like this:

Can you buy some fruit?
Yes, of course.

Can you buy some…?
Yes, of course.

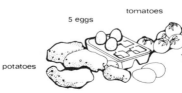

2 bread

3 meat

4 fish

cheese

1 fruit

shampoo

soap

toothpaste

cigarettes

writing paper

pens

tomatoes

5 eggs

potatoes

stamps

envelopes

Can you open the window? Yes, O.K.

Can you close the door? I'm sorry, I can't just now.

2. Ask and answer like this:
Can you open the door?
Yes, O.K. *or* I'm sorry, I can't just now.

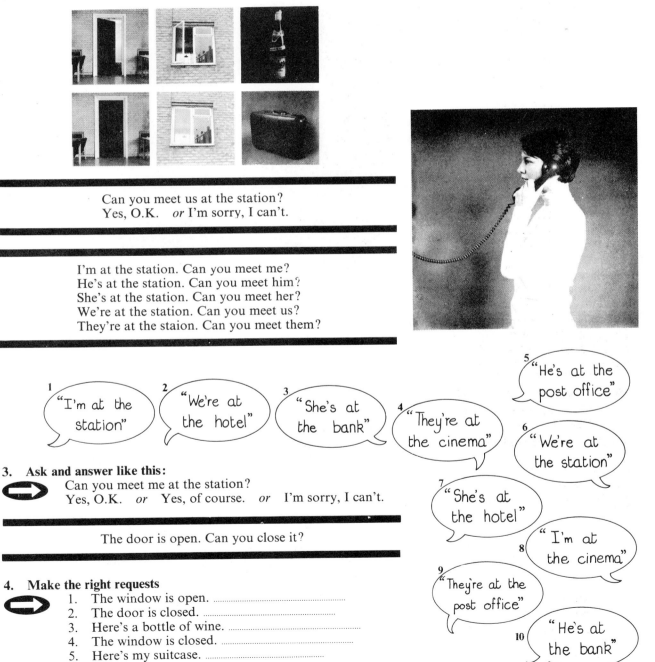

Can you meet us at the station?
Yes, O.K. *or* I'm sorry, I can't.

I'm at the station. Can you meet me?
He's at the station. Can you meet him?
She's at the station. Can you meet her?
We're at the station. Can you meet us?
They're at the staion. Can you meet them?

1 "I'm at the station"
2 "We're at the hotel"
3 "She's at the bank"
4 "They're at the cinema"
5 "He's at the post office"
6 "We're at the station"
7 "She's at the hotel"
8 "I'm at the cinema"
9 "They're at the post office"
10 "He's at the bank"

3. Ask and answer like this:
Can you meet me at the station?
Yes, O.K. *or* Yes, of course. *or* I'm sorry, I can't.

The door is open. Can you close it?

4. Make the right requests
1. The window is open. ....
2. The door is closed. ....
3. Here's a bottle of wine. ....
4. The window is closed. ....
5. Here's my suitcase. ....
6. The door is open. ....

UNIT 14

At the greengrocer's

MAN: **Yes, can I help you?**

JACKIE: **Yes, I'd like some fruit, please.**

MAN: **What would you like?**

JACKIE: **I'd like some oranges please.**

MAN: **How many would you like?**

JACKIE: **Three please. And some of those apples.**

MAN: **Which ones would you like?**

JACKIE: **Those ones over there – the Granny Smiths. Three of them.**

MAN: **Right. That's 44 pence please... Lovely day, isn't it?**

JACKIE: **Yes, beautiful. Thank you very much. Goodbye.**

MAN: **Goodbye.**

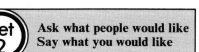

Set 2   Ask what people would like
Say what you would like

1. **Look at the things to buy on page 76. Ask and answer like this:**
   What would you like?
   I'd like some fruit please.

   What would you like?
   I'd like .... please.

2. **Look at the things again. Ask and answer like this:**
   Can you do some shopping for me?
   Yes, of course. What would you like?
   I'd like some fruit and some bread please *or*
   I'd like some soap and some toothpaste please.

   Choose 2 things that you would like each time

I'd like some oranges please. How many would you like?

3. Ask and answer like this:

   I'd like some .... please.
How many would you like?
I'd like .... please.

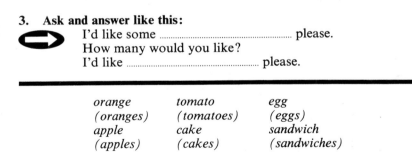

orange	*tomato*	*egg*
(oranges)	*(tomatoes)*	*(eggs)*
apple	*cake*	*sandwich*
(apples)	*(cakes)*	*(sandwiches)*

Set 3 — **Ask for and give specific information**

Can I have an orange please?
Yes – which one would you like?
This one.

Can I have an apple please?
Yes – which one would you like?
That one over there.

1. Look at the things to eat above. Ask and answer like this:

   Can I have a/an .... please?
Yes – which one would you like?
This one/That one over there.

I'd like some oranges please.
Yes – which ones would you like?
These ones.

I'd like some apples please.
Yes – which ones would you like?
Those ones over there.

2. Look at the things to eat again. Ask and answer like this:

   I'd like some .... please.
Yes ....
These ones/Those ones over there.

Set 4 — Talk about the weather

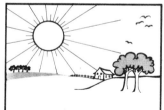

lovely
beautiful

awful
terrible

Ask and answer like this:

Lovely day, isn't it?
Yes, beautiful.

Terrible day, isn't it?
Yes, ...

EXTENSION

1.  **A note from Tessa to David**

David,
I to my late evening
today. Can you do some
shopping? I think I'd like
some fish for supper.
Oh — and can you buy
some more soap and
some toothpaste? See
you at about 6.30.

Tessa.

**Write a note like this to a
friend. Say what you would
like your friend to buy and say what
time you will be back.**

2. Group work
**Work in groups of 4–5. You go with some friends to a restaurant for
dinner. Here is the menu. One of you is the waiter and asks what
everybody would like. Answer like this:**

I'd like some ...., then some ....
and then some ....

- - - - - _Menu_ - - - -

Egg Mayonnaise
Orange Juice
· · · · · · · · · · · · ·
Chicken Salad   Vegetables
Grilled Fish   ─ ─ ─ ─ ─ ─
Roast Beef   Potatoes
                  Peas
                  Tomatoes
· · · · · · · · · · · · · · · ·
Fresh Fruit
Ice Cream
Cheese and Biscuits
· · · · · · · · · · · · · · · · ·

3. **Murray, Neville and Jackie are in the restaurant car on the train back to Manchester. Listen to them talking and write down what each of them has to eat and drink**

	To eat	To drink
Murray	....	....
Neville	....	....
Jackie	....	....

OPEN DIALOGUE

You are having dinner with Murray. Look at the menu on page 80.

MURRAY: Well, here's the menu... let's see... there's chicken, fish and roast beef. Do you like fish?

STUDENT: ....

MURRAY: Or what about chicken? Would you like some chicken salad?

STUDENT: ....

MURRAY: All right. And what about vegetables?

STUDENT: ....

MURRAY: Fine. And what would you like after that – fresh fruit, or ice cream, or cheese and biscuits?

STUDENT: ....

MURRAY: And to drink?

STUDENT: ....

MURRAY: Right. I'll order.

ORAL EXERCISES

1. Ask people what they would like. Look at the food on page 76

What would you like? Would you like some fruit?
Yes, please.

What would you like? Would you like some bread?
No, thank you.

2. Offer people things and ask them to buy them. Look at the food again

Would you like some fruit for lunch?
Yes, please.
Well, can you buy some?

Would you like some bread for lunch?
Yes, please.
Well, can you buy some?

3. Say what you would like. Jackie is going to the shops

What sort of fruit would you like, apples or oranges?
I'd like some apples <u>and</u> some oranges.

And would you like meat or fish?
I'd like some meat <u>and</u> some fish.

4. Ask somebody to meet you and your friends

Your train arrives at 10.
Can you meet me at the station.

Her plane arrives at 9.
Can you meet her at the airport.

5. Ask for specific information

Can I have an apple?
Yes, which one would you like?

I'd like some eggs.
Yes, which ones would you like?

6. Give specific information

Which apples would you like? These ones?
No, those ones over there.

Which cake would you like? That one?
No, this one.

REMEMBER

This is how you:

1. Ask somebody to do something

Can you buy some fruit?
Can you open the window?
Can you meet me at the station?

2. Agree to do something

Yes, of course.
Yes, O.K.

3. Say you can't do things.

I'm sorry, I can't (just now).

4. Ask what people would like

What would you like?

5. Say what you would like

I'd like some { fish, please.
                 oranges

6. Ask for and give specific information

Which one/ones would you like?
This one/That one over there.
These ones/Those ones over there.

7. Make remarks about the weather

Lovely day, isn't it?
Yes, beautiful.

8. Thank people informally

Thanks!

Grammar

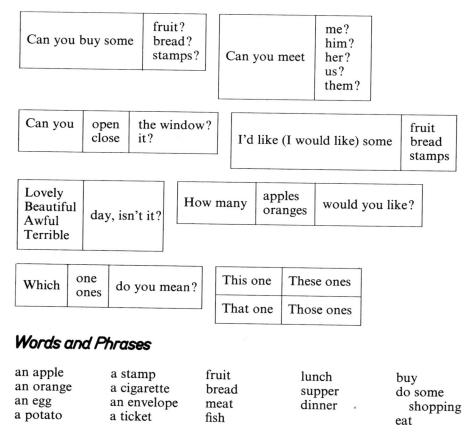

Can you buy some	fruit? bread? stamps?

Can you meet	me? him? her? us? them?

Can you	open close	the window? it?

I'd like (I would like) some	fruit bread stamps

Lovely Beautiful Awful Terrible	day, isn't it?

How many	apples oranges	would you like?

Which	one ones	do you mean?

This one	These ones
That one	Those ones

Words and Phrases

an apple	a stamp	fruit	lunch	buy	open
an orange	a cigarette	bread	supper	do some	closed
an egg	an envelope	meat	dinner	shopping	lovely
a potato	a ticket	fish		eat	beautiful
a tomato	a pen	cheese		pack up	awful
	a menu	vegetables		mean	terrible
				open	
	a door	soap		close	which
	a window	toothpaste		drink	how many?
	a suitcase	shampoo			thanks!
	a bottle			at	all right!
	a day				ready?
					then

Happy Birthday

In the cafeteria at Focus Films

MURRAY: **It's Tessa's birthday soon.**
ALLAN: **Oh, when is it?**
MURRAY: **It's on January the tenth.**
JACKIE: **That's on Monday!**
MURRAY: **Yes, that's right.**

 Ask and talk about dates

Days of the week	Months of the year		Dates			
Monday	January	July	1st = first		16th = sixteenth	
Tuesday	February	August	2nd = second		17th = seventeenth, etc.	
Wednesday	March	September	3rd = third			
Thursday	April	October	4th = fourth		20th = twentieth	
Friday	May	November	5th = fifth		21st = twenty-first, etc.	
Saturday	June	December	6th = sixth			
Sunday			7th = seventh		30th = thirtieth	
			8th = eighth		31st = thirty-first, etc.	
			9th = ninth			
			10th = tenth			
			11th = eleventh			
			12th = twelfth			
			13th = thirteenth			
			14th = fourteenth			
			15th = fifteenth			

When's Tessa's birthday? It's on January the tenth (January 10th)

1. **Ask and answer like this:**
    When's Tessa's birthday?
    It's on January the tenth.

    When's Murray's birthday?
    It's on ....

FOCUS FILMS – BIRTHDAYS

TESSA	— JANUARY 10TH	NEVILLE	— FEBRUARY 27TH
JACKIE	— APRIL 1ST	ALLAN	— MAY 2ND
MURRAY	— NOVEMBER 14TH	SHEILA	— DECEMBER 5TH
GEORGE	— JULY 3RD		

UNIT 15

January the tenth is a Monday.

January
Monday
10

10-355 Week 2

January						February					
Mon		3	10	17	24	31	Mon		7	14	21	28
Tue		4	11	18	25		Tue	1	8	15	22	
Wed		5	12	19	26		Wed	2	9	16	23	
Thu		6	13	20	27		Thu	3	10	17	24	
Fri		7	14	21	28		Fri	4	11	18	25	
Sat	1	8	15	22	29		Sat	5	12	19	26	

2. **Look at a diary for this year. Look at the Focus birthday dates and say what day of the week they are, like this:**

    January the tenth is a . . .

April the first is a . . .

Tessa's birthday is on January 10th.
That's on Monday!
Yes, that's right.

3. **Make statements like this about the birthdays of the people at Focus Films. Say the days of the week from Exercise 2**

    Murray's birthday is on . . .
That's on _____
Yes, that's right.

4. **Ask your partner when his/her birthday is, like this:**

    When's your birthday?
It's on _____

Then tell the class:
(Peter's) birthday is on . . .

5. **Write the answers to these questions:**
1. What date is it today?
2. What date is it tomorrow?
3. What day is it today?
4. What day is it tomorrow?
5. When is your birthday?
6. When is your partner's birthday?
7. When is your teacher's birthday?
8. When is your next English lesson?

ALLAN:	What shall we give her?
MURRAY:	Let's give her some chocolates.
JACKIE:	No, not chocolates. Let's give her some flowers.
MURRAY:	Yes, that's a good idea.

On January 10th

TESSA:	Good morning, everyone! Awful day, isn't it?
MURRAY:	Yes, terrible! But it's your birthday, Tessa. Happy Birthday!
TESSA:	Oh, thanks. Oh, what beautiful flowers! Are they from you, Murray?
MURRAY:	They're from all of us.
TESSA:	Well, thank you very much, all of you. They're lovely!

Set 2 — Ask for suggestions   Agree with suggestions
Make suggestions   Disagree with suggestions

What shall we give her?
Let's give her some chocolates.
Yes, that's a good idea.
No, not chocolates.

1. **Ask and answer like this:**

It's Tessa's birthday tomorrow. What shall we give her?
Let's give her some _____ /a _____
Yes, that's a good idea./No, not (a) _____ Let's give her _____
or
It's Murray's birthday tomorrow. What shall we give him?
Let's give him some _____ /a _____
Yes, that's a good idea./No, not (a) _____ Let's give him _____

PRESENTS

some flowers	*a record*
some chocolates	*a book*
some perfume	*a bottle of whisky*
some aftershave	*a poster*
some glasses	*a T-shirt*
some plates	

2. Decide what to give these people for their birthdays

TESSA: ....

MURRAY: ....

ALLAN: ....

NEVILLE: ....

JACKIE: ....

Now practise making the suggestions with a partner, like this:

➡ It's ....'s birthday tomorrow.
Let's give him/her ....
That's a good idea./No, not ....Let's give him/her ....

IDEAS

| go to a cafe | go to the beach | go out for a meal | go home | watch TV |
| 1 go to the cinema | 2 go to the club | 3 go out for a walk | 4 have a party | 5 stay at home |

What shall we do?
Let's go to the cinema.
Yes, that's a good idea./No, let's go to the cafe

3. Ask and answer like this:

➡ What shall we do?
Let's go to the cinema.
Yes, that's a good idea./No, let's ....

What shall we do?
Let's ....
Yes, that's a good idea./No, let's ....

What shall we do on Friday evening?   Let's go out for a meal.

4. Work with a partner. Make suggestions for the times below. Ask and answer like this:

➡ What shall we do on ....
Let's ....
Yes, that's a ..../No, let's ....

Tuesday evening   *Saturday afternoon*   *Sunday morning*
Friday evening   *Saturday evening*

Set 3 Express pleasure

1. Express pleasure like this:
➡ What an interesting book!
What a lovely film!
What a(n) ....!

a book	*a record*	*a poster*
a film	*a man*	*a T–shirt*
a house	*a girl*	
a room	*a garden*	

2. Now express pleasure like this:
➡ What beautiful flowers!
What lovely glasses!
What ....!

flowers
plates
glasses
posters
people
chocolates

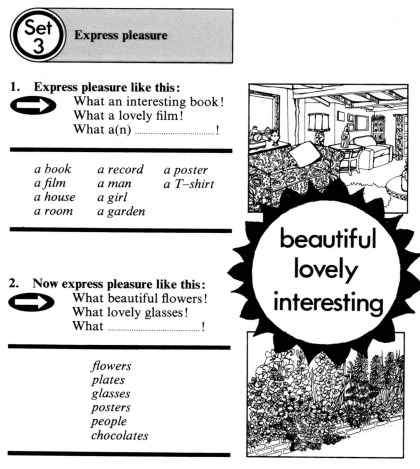

beautiful
lovely
interesting

Festivals, Parties and Presents

The two important religious festivals in England are Christmas and Easter. On December 25th, Christmas Day, families and friends meet and give presents. On Easter Sunday, people give chocolate eggs, chocolates and flowers. Many people also eat eggs for breakfast on Easter Day.

Another big festival is Bonfire Night. This festival celebrates the day when a man called Guy Fawkes was caught when he tried to blow up the Houses of Parliament in London. This was November 5th, 1605. Now, every November 5th, children and adults light bonfires, burn a 'guy' (a 'man' made of sticks and old clothes) and light fireworks.

There are special customs for giving presents in England. Only a member of a family can give a present of money but a friend can give a record token, a book token or a gift token to spend in a big shop.

When you go to dinner or a party in a friend's home, you can give a small present if you like: some chocolates, some flowers or something to drink, like a bottle of wine.

EXTENSION

1. Tessa writes a letter to thank a friend for a birthday present

> Dear Simon,
> Thank you very much for the beautiful glasses. They are lovely. David and I are always breaking glasses so we never have enough.
> Love
> Tessa

Write the first part of the letter to 4 people you know. Thank them for some of the presents above or other presents you would like. You can finish your letter with *yours* or *love* and your name

2.

3. Listen to Tessa and David talking about David's mother's birthday. Write down when her birthday is, what they decide to give her and what they decide to do.
Date of birthday:.........................
Present:.........................
Outing: What?.........................
When?.........................

OPEN DIALOGUE

It's Saturday afternoon. You meet Tessa

TESSA: Beautiful day, isn't it?
STUDENT: ....
TESSA: What shall we do?
STUDENT: ....
TESSA: Good idea. Come on then. When's your birthday by the way?
STUDENT: ....
TESSA: Oh, is it? What shall we do on your birthday?
STUDENT: ....
TESSA: Mmm, all right. Oh, it's Murray's birthday on November 14th. What shall we give him?
STUDENT: ....
TESSA: Yes, that's a good idea. Let's give him that. I'll tell the others.

ORAL EXERCISES

1. **Say when people's birthdays are. Look at page 83**
When's Tessa's birthday?
It's on January 10th.

When's Jackie's birthday?
It's on April 1st.

2. **Say what month people's birthdays are. Look at the list of birthdays again**
Is Tessa's birthday in March?
No, it's in January.

Is Jackie's birthday in May?
No, it's in April.

3. **Agree with suggestions**
What shall we give him? A record?
Yes, that's a good idea. Let's give him a record.

What shall we give her? Some flowers?
Yes, that's a good idea. Let's give her some flowers.

4. **Suggest things to do. Look at page 85**
What shall we do? Shall we go to the cinema?
Yes, that's a good idea.

What shall we do? Shall we go to the club?
Yes, that's a good idea.

5. **Express pleasure when people give or show you things**
Do you like the flowers?
Yes, I do. They're beautiful!

Do you like my room?
Yes, I do. It's beautiful!

6. **Disagree with these suggestions**
Let's go to the cinema tonight.
No, not the cinema!

Well, shall we go to London?
No, not London!

REMEMBER

This is how you:
1. Ask about dates   When's Tessa's birthday?
2. Talk about dates   It's on January the tenth.
                                  It's on Monday.
                                  January the tenth is a Monday.
3. Ask for suggestions   What shall we give her?
                                  What shall we do?
4. Make suggestions   Let's give her some flowers.
                                  Let's go to the cinema.
5. Agree with suggestions   Yes, that's a good idea!
6. Disagree with suggestions No, not flowers.
7. Express pleasure   What a lovely room!
                                  What beautiful flowers!
8. Thank people for things Thank you for the beautiful flowers.

Grammar

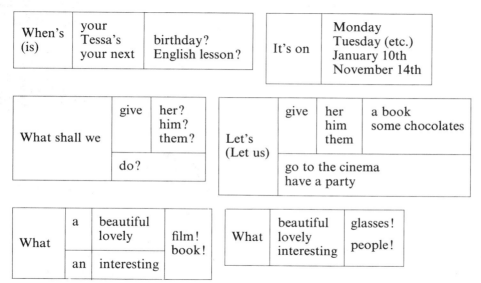

When's (is)	your Tessa's your next	birthday? English lesson?

It's on	Monday Tuesday (etc.) January 10th November 14th

What shall we	give	her? him? them?
	do?	

Let's (Let us)	give	her him them	a book some chocolates
	go to the cinema have a party		

What	a	beautiful lovely	film! book!
	an	interesting	

What	beautiful lovely interesting	glasses! people!

Words and Phrases

Days of the week
  (Monday, Tuesday, etc.)
Months of the year
  (January, February, etc.)
Ordinal numbers
  (1st, 2nd, etc.)

today
tomorrow

a year
a television

a date
a birthday
a flower
a book
a plate
a poster
a T–shirt
a meal
a walk
a party
a man
a family

people

chocolate
perfume
aftershave

interesting
different

That's a good idea
Happy Birthday!

next
also

go to . . .
go out for . . .
give
watch TV
  (television)
stay at home
try

A nice weekend

It's Friday night. Murray and Anna Freeman decide to go to London for the weekend. They drive down to London on Saturday morning and they stop for lunch in a pub on the way. In the afternoon they do some shopping and go and see some friends who live in West London. They decide to go to the theatre in the evening. Their friends say the musical, Evita, is very good, but the tickets are very expensive. In the end, they go to see The Mousetrap, an old Agatha Christie play. They stay the night with their friends and on Sunday morning they go for a walk in Hyde Park. In the afternoon they go to an exhibition at the Tate Gallery. Then after tea with their friends, they drive back to Manchester and get back home late on Sunday evening. On Monday morning Murray is very tired and is a little late for work.

Monday morning at work.
> (Murray yawns)

TESSA: **What's the matter Murray? Are you tired?**

MURRAY: **Yes, I am. Do you know what I want to do—I want to go home, go to bed and go back to sleep.**

TESSA: **But it's only a quarter past nine. Did you have a nice weekend?**

MURRAY: **Yes thanks, we did.**

TESSA: **What did you do?**

MURRAY: **We went to London and saw some friends—and we went to the theatre on Saturday night.**

TESSA: **Oh, what did you see?**

MURRAY: **Don't laugh—but we saw the Mousetrap!**

TESSA: **The Agatha Christie play? Did you? What was it like?**

MURRAY: **It was quite good. Just a detective story. We wanted to see the musical about Eva Peron, but the tickets cost £5 each! So we didn't go.**

TESSA: **Oh, what a pity! I want to see that too. Well, I did nothing all weekend. I was ill in bed. We went to a fish and chip bar on Friday night. I expect it was that.**

MURRAY: **Oh, what did you have to eat?**

TESSA: **Fish and chips, of course! Well, Murray, it's half-past nine. It's time . . .**

MURRAY: **. . . for a cup of strong, black coffee. I'll make it!**

UNIT 16

Set 1 — Ask people what they want to do.
Say what you want to do.

Set 2 — Ask and talk about the past

I want to go home.

---

1. You are bored. Say what you want to do.
Work with a partner, like this:

 I'm bored. I want to go to the club.
That's a good idea. I'm bored too.

2. You are tired. Say what you want to do.
Work with a partner, like this:

 I'm tired. I want to go home.
That's a good idea. I'm tired too.

Bored	**Tired**

go to the club	*go home*
go to the beach	*sit down*
go to the cinema	*sit down and read*
go out for a walk	*sit down and watch TV*
go out for a drink	*go to bed*
go and see some friends	*go to bed and read*
invite some friends to supper	*go to sleep*
have a party	*stay at home*

What do you want to do? I want to go to the club.

---

3. Ask and answer like this:

 I'm bored. I want to go to the club. What
do you want to do?
I want to go to the club too.
or
I'm tired. I want to go home. What do
you want to do?
I want to go home too.

4. Ask your partner what he/she wants to do after the class, like this:

 What do you want to do after the class . . . ?
I want to ....

Set 2 — Ask and talk about the past

YESTERDAY	LAST WEEK
yesterday morning	on Monday
yesterday afternoon	on Tuesday etc.
yesterday evening	on Wednesday evening
last night	at the weekend

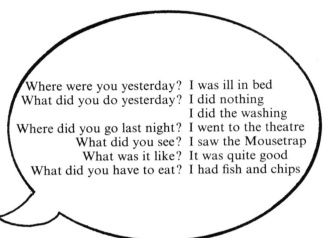

Where were you yesterday? I was ill in bed
What did you do yesterday? I did nothing
I did the washing
Where did you go last night? I went to the theatre
What did you see? I saw the Mousetrap
What was it like? It was quite good
What did you have to eat? I had fish and chips

Where were you yesterday? I was at home.

---

1. Ask and answer like this:

 Where were you yesterday?
I was ....

in bed	*at home*	*at work*
ill	*in London*	*in town*

What was the film like? It was good.

---

2. Ask and answer like this:

 What was the film like?
It was ....

(quite) interesting	*(quite) good*	*awful*
beautiful	*terrible*	*all right*

What did you do yesterday? I did the washing.

3. Ask and answer like this:

➡️ What did you do yesterday?
I did ....

my homework	*the ironing*	*the shopping*
the housework	*the washing*	*the garden*

Where did you go yesterday? I went to the cinema.

4. Ask and answer like this:

➡️ Where did you go yesterday?
I went to ....

the cinema	*a friend's house*	*work*
the beach		*college*
the club		*town*

What did you see? I saw The Mousetrap.

5. Ask and answer like this:

➡️ What did you see?
I saw ....

The Carlton Affair	*the news*	*a documentary film about people at work*
King Kong	*a French film*	
The Tower of London	*Big Ben*	*a variety programme*

What did you have for breakfast?
I had a cup of coffee.

6. Ask and answer like this:

➡️ What did you have for breakfast?
I had a .... and ....

a cup of tea	*some bread and butter*
a cup of coffee	*some toast*
a glass of milk	*an egg*
a glass of orange juice	*a cheese sandwich*

7. Now ask your partner these questions:

➡️ What did you have for breakfast yesterday?
What did you have for lunch yesterday?
What did you do last night?
What did you see on television?
What was it like?
When did you go to bed?

EXTENSION

1. Jackie writes her diary for last weekend

Saturday 8th — Went shopping in the morning. Saw Neville and Maria. Had lunch at an old pub outside Manchester. Did some housework in the afternoon. Went to see King Kong with Allan in the evening. Went to his flat after the film and had coffee. Back home at 1 a.m.! Allan wants to go to Madeira with me in July. Don't want to go — What shall I say to him?

Sunday 9th — Got up late. Went out for a walk. Washed my hair after lunch and did some ironing. Watched an old Hitchkock film on TV in the evening — it was very good. Went to bed early.

Now write your own diary for last weekend. Say what you did, where you went, what you saw, what time you got up or went to bed

2. George and Doris Blake went to Madeira for a holiday in January. Doris wrote this post-card to some friends

Madeira

Post Card

Having a lovely time!
It's quite hot —
George went swimming
yesterday but I didn't.
Went sightseeing in
the town on Wed. and
saw a lovely old church.
Went to a nice
restaurant last night
and had 'paella' —
very tasty! See you
next week,
Regards
Doris and George

Mr & Mrs J. Thomas,
45 Grange Road,
Manchester,
ENGLAND.

3. 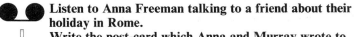 **Listen to Anna Freeman talking to a friend about their holiday in Rome.**
Write the post-card which Anna and Murray wrote to Tessa and David at the end of their holiday

Post Card

Mr and Mrs D Richards
54 Garden Walk,
Manchester
ENGLAND

OPEN DIALOGUE

Talk to Jackie

JACKIE: Hello! How are you?
STUDENT: ....
JACKIE: Oh, fine thanks. Did you have a nice weekend?
STUDENT: ....
JACKIE: What did you do? Where did you go?
STUDENT: ....
JACKIE: What did you see on TV—a film? The news?
STUDENT: ....
JACKIE: You sound tired—what time did you go to bed last night?
STUDENT: ....
JACKIE: Well, I went to bed at two, and I didn't have any breakfast this morning. What did you have?
STUDENT: ....
JACKIE: Mm, that sounds good! Well, I must go and get a cup of coffee. Bye!
STUDENT: ....

ORAL EXERCISES

1. Ask people about the past
Ask Murray if he had a nice weekend.
Did you have a nice weekend, Murray?

Ask Tessa if she had a nice evening.
Did you have a nice evening, Tessa?

2. Ask people about the past again
Ask Murray what he did yesterday.
What did you do yesterday, Murray?

Ask Tessa where she went yesterday.
Where did you go yesterday, Tessa?

3. Ask people to repeat statements
I went to the cinema last night.
Sorry! Where did you go?

I did my homework yesterday.
Sorry! What did you do?

4. Say what people did in the past. Answer these questions from the dialogue
Where did Murray and Anna go on Saturday (which town)?
They went to London.

Who did they see?
They saw some friends.

5. Ask what people want to do. Look at page 90
I'm bored.
Do you want to go to the club?

She's bored.
Does she want to go to the beach?

6. Say what you want to do. Look at page 90.
What's the matter?
I'm tired. I want to go home.

What's the matter?
I'm tired. I want to sit down and read.

REMEMBER

This is how you:
1. Ask people what they want to do   What do you want to do?
2. Say what you want to do   I want to go to the cinema.
3. Ask about the past   Where were you yesterday?
    What did you do yesterday?
    Where did you go?
    What did you see?
    What was it like?
4. Talk about the past   I was at home.
    I went to London.
    I did the washing.
    I saw 'The Carlton Affair'.
    I had a cup of coffee.
    It was quite good.

Grammar

What	do	you they	want to do?
	does	he she	

I We They	want	to	go home
He She	wants		invite some friends to dinner

What	did	you he she	do? see? have?
Where		they	go?

I He She We They	did	(my) homework
	saw	a film
	had	a sandwich
	went	to London

Where	was	John? Mary?
	were	you? your friends?

He She I	was	at home ill in London
We They	were	

What	was	the film book	like?
		it	

It	was	good awful interesting

Words and Phrases

a theatre
a musical

the news
a variety programme
a documentary film

a post-card
a holiday
a church

the washing
the shopping

chips
butter
toast

weekend
yesterday
last night
last week

quite

ill
bored
tired
old

want (wanted)
invite (invited)
sit down (sat)
go to sleep (went)
go home
see (saw)
yawn (yawned)
stop (stopped)
say (said)
find (found)

don't laugh!
what's the matter?
who?

An Invitation

JACKIE:	**872 4679. Hello?**
ALLAN:	**Is that Jackie?**
JACKIE:	**Yes, speaking.**
ALLAN:	**Hello, it's Allan here.**
JACKIE:	**Oh, hello Allan! How are you?**
ALLAN:	**Fine thanks! And you?**
JACKIE:	**Oh, all right.**
ALLAN:	**I didn't see you at work today.**
JACKIE:	**No, I wasn't well. I was at home but I'm all right now.**
ALLAN:	**Oh good. Listen, are you free on Thursday evening?**
JACKIE:	**No, I'm afraid I'm not.**
ALLAN:	**Oh, what a pity! What about this evening? Are you free this evening?**
JACKIE:	**Yes, I am. Why?**

 Set 1

Answer the telephone
Say your name on the telephone
Start a conversation

872 4679 Hello?   Is that Jackie?
Yes, speaking.   Hello, it's Allan here.

1. Roleplaying
Work in pairs. Take both parts in turn.

Murray rings Tessa. Tessa's telephone number is 354 5223.
Neville rings Maria. Maria's telephone number is 477 9372.
George rings Murray. Murray's telephone number is 678 1013.

How are you?
Fine thanks! And you?
Oh, all right.

2. Practise this exchange with your partner

3. Telephone your partner: remember what you practised in Exercises 1 and 2

UNIT 17

Are you free on Thursday evening?	No, I'm afraid I'm not.
Are you free this evening?	Yes, I am.

Today	*Tomorrow*	*Thursday*
this morning	tomorrow morning	on Thursday morning
this afternoon	tomorrow afternoon	on Thursday afternoon
this evening	tomorrow evening	on Thursday evening
tonight	tomorrow night	on Thursday night

**Martha is a doctor. She works in a hospital.
This is her diary for the week.**

Diary

MONDAY
Hospital 8 a.m. – 4 p.m.

TUESDAY
night duty 8 p.m. – 8 a.m.

WEDNESDAY
free
7 p.m. see Ann

THURSDAY
hospital 8 a.m. – 4 p.m.

FRIDAY
hospital 8 a.m. – 4 p.m.
cinema 7.15 p.m. – Peter

SATURDAY
shopping in morning
hospital 6 p.m. – 1 a.m.

SUNDAY
lunch with Mother

**1. Work in pairs. One of you is
Martha. Ask Martha if she is free at
these times:**

> *Monday evening*
> *Tuesday evening*
> *Wednesday afternoon*
> *Wednesday evening*
> *Thursday morning*
> *Friday evening*
> *Saturday afternoon*
> *Sunday at lunchtime*
> *Sunday evening*

Ask and answer like this:

> Are you free on Monday
> evening?
> Yes, I am.
> Oh good! Are you free on
> Tuesday evening?
> No, I'm afraid I'm not.
> What a pity!
> Are you free on ....

2. Write a diary like Martha's for yourself

**3. Work in pairs, with your diaries. Ask your partner if he/she is free
at these times:**

1. *this evening*	5. *on Saturday afternoon*
2. *tomorrow morning*	6. *on Saturday evening*
3. *tomorrow afternoon*	7. *on Sunday evening*
4. *tomorrow night*	

ALLAN: Well, would you like to go to the cinema tonight?

JACKIE: Yes, I'd love to. What a lovely idea!

ALLAN: What would you like to see? The Carlton Affair? Single Ticket to Death?

JACKIE: No, not Single Ticket to Death. I saw that last year. It's an old film. Let's go and see The Carlton Affair. What time does it start?

ALLAN: Let's see… er… it starts at 8.30. It's at the Odeon cinema.

JACKIE: Well, where shall we meet and when?

ALLAN: Let's meet outside the cinema just before eight thirty.

JACKIE: All right. See you then. Thanks for ringing. Bye!

ALLAN: Bye! See you later.

Set 3

Invite people to do things
Accept invitations to do things
Refuse invitations to do things

Would you like to go to the cinema tonight?
Yes, I'd love to. *or*
Sorry, I'm afraid I can't.

---

1. Ask and answer like this:

➡ Would you like to go to the cinema tomorrow?
Yes, I'd love to. *or* Sorry, I'm afraid I can't.
Would you like to ....?

....

---

go to the cinema	*go out for a meal*	*come to lunch*
go to the beach	*go out for a drink*	*come to dinner*
go to the club	*go out for a walk*	*come to my house*
go to a disco		

---

2. Joe telephones Maria, but she's out. So he writes her a note. Write invitations to three friends inviting them to:

1. *The cinema/Friday evening/King Kong*
2. *Dinner/Saturday evening*
3. *A meal/tomorrow evening*

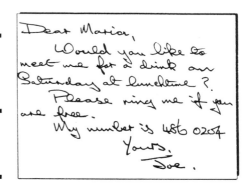

3. Roleplaying
Work in pairs. Telephone your partner and:
1. Ask if he or she is free on Saturday evening
2. Invite him or her to go to the cinema to see a James Bond film
3. Suggest that you go out for a meal *after* the film
4. Suggest that you meet outside the cinema at 7.00 p.m
5. Say goodbye

4. Now do the same with a real film, a real cinema, a real restaurant, and suggest a real place to meet

EXTENSION

Let's go to the Cinema tonight!

What's on in Manchester this week Jan 15th-21st

		Times of Performances
Odeon	The Carlton Affair (AA)	
Plaza	Single Ticket to Death (X)	
Cinecenter	Modern Life (A)	
ABC	Child of the Dogs (U)	
The Classic	Passing Trains (AA)	

1. Listen to the girl on the telephone giving information about these films. Write in the *times* of the performances for each film

2. Write your answer to Murray's invitation:
1. Accept or refuse the invitation
2. Ask if he's free to come to a small party at your flat or house (say when it is)

Look at Julian's letter if you need some help

Julian

You are invited to a party

on Friday, December 7th

at 8.30 p.m.

at
3 Carlton Walk, Manchester 8

Please bring a bottle

Murray Freeman

R.S.V.P.

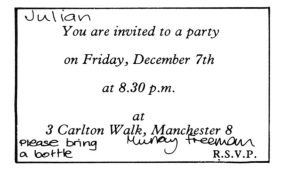

43, Addison Gardens,
Manchester.
Nov. 30th.

Dear Murray,
Thanks for your invitation to the party on Friday - Yes, I'd love to come.
By the way, are you and Anna free on Saturday (Dec. 15th)? If you are, would you like to come to dinner at my flat? Very informal, just one or two good friends - I hope you can come.
See you on Friday,
Yours,
Julian.

3. **Listen to the students' meeting at the college.**
Answer these questions
1. What event at the college is the student announcing?
2. When is it? What time of day?
3. How much are the tickets?
4. Who must you see if you would like to go?
5. When must you see her?

OPEN DIALOGUE

Look at the cinema programme on page 98.
Your telephone is ringing. Answer it
Brrr! Brrr! Brrr!

STUDENT: ....

MURRAY: Hello! It's Murray here.

STUDENT: ....

MURRAY: How are you?

STUDENT: ....

MURRAY: Oh, I'm all right. Did you have a nice weekend?

STUDENT: ....

MURRAY: Look, are you free this week on Friday or Saturday evening?

STUDENT: ....

MURRAY: Oh, good! Well, would you like to go to the cinema?

STUDENT: ....

MURRAY: Well, have a look at the programmes. What would you like to see?

STUDENT: ....

MURRAY: Mmm! All right. That sounds good. What time would you like to go?

STUDENT: ....

MURRAY: All right. Shall I meet you at your house?

STUDENT: ....

MURRAY: Oh, wait a moment! Where do you live? I don't remember.

STUDENT: ....

MURRAY: Oh, yes, of course. What time shall I come?

STUDENT: ....

MURRAY: All right. I'll see you then. Bye!

STUDENT: ....

ORAL EXERCISES

1. Ask people if they are free
Ask Murray if he's free on Wednesday morning
Are you free on Wednesday morning, Murray?

See if Sally is free tomorrow evening
Are you free tomorrow evening, Sally?

2. Say when you are free. Look at Martha's diary
Are you free on Monday evening?
Monday evening? Yes, I am.

Are you free on Tuesday evening?
Tuesday evening? No, I'm afraid I'm not.

3. Invite people to do things. Look at page 97
Choose something suitable
I'm free this evening.
Oh, would you like to...

What shall we do on Saturday afternoon?
Would you like to . . .

4. Accept or refuse invitations
Would you like to go to the cinema tonight?
Yes, I'd love to.

Would you like to go to the cinema tonight?
No, I'm afraid I can't.

Accept or refuse the invitations as you wish

5. What would you say?
How are you?
Fine thanks. And you?
I'm sorry, I can't come to the cinema with you tonight.
Oh, what a pity!
But I can come to your birthday party.

....

And I wondered if you would like to come to the football match with me on Saturday.

....

And are you free for lunch some day next week?

....

O.K.—let's meet then, but anyway I'll see you at your birthday party on Sunday.

....

UNIT 17

REMEMBER

This is how you:

1.	Answer the telephone	872 4679 Hello?
		Yes, speaking.
2.	Say your name on the telephone	It's Allan here.
3.	Start a conversation	How are you?
		Fine thanks! And you?
		Not too bad.
4.	Arrange to meet somebody	Are you free tomorrow evening?
		Yes I am.
		No, I'm afraid I'm not.
5.	Invite people to do things	Would you like to go to the cinema?
6.	Accept invitations to do things	Yes, I'd love to.
7.	Refuse invitations to do things	Sorry, I'm afraid I can't.
8.	Say you are pleased	Oh good!
9.	Say you are disappointed	Oh, what a pity!
10.	Make parting remarks	Bye! See you later.

Grammar

On	Monday Tuesday Wednesday	morning afternoon evening
This Tomorrow		

Would you like to	go	to the cinema? to the theatre? out for a meal? out for a drink? out for a walk?
	come	to lunch? to dinner?
I'd (I would) love to.		

Words and Phrases

a night	tonight	before	ring (rang)	why?
a diary	this (evening)	after	come (came)	speaking
an invitation	lunchtime		bring (brought)	how are you?
		well		fine, thanks!
football		free		What a pity!
				Oh good!
				I'd love to
				See you (on Friday)
				wait a moment

Going to work

And how long does it take?

Er... let's see... It usually takes about twenty-five minutes. That's in the rush-hour, of course.

(from the Manchester News)

Manchester Traffic Problem Increases

An accident in the centre of Manchester on Friday night brought traffic to a standstill for one hour. One motorist left his office at 6 o'clock and got home at half-past eight. He lives seven miles away. Asked why he did not turn around and try another route, he answered: 'There is only one route through the centre of Manchester. It's all one way now!'

The traffic problem is the same in the rush hour. 'The only people who get to work on time are cyclists,' said another angry motorist. 'If Manchester Council doesn't improve the traffic system I shall buy a bicycle.'

Mr J. H. Jones, from the Manchester Council made this comment: 'The one-way system is all right; it's the number of motorists that's wrong. It's a mystery to me why more people don't leave their cars at home and travel by train or cycle to work.'

Sally Baker is writing an article on car pollution. She asks some people at Focus Films about their journey to work.

MURRAY: Hello Sally. I saw your article yesterday in the Manchester News. It was very good.

SALLY: Oh thanks. Well, I'm writing another one now. Can you answer some questions?

MURRAY: Er... Yes... What about?

SALLY: About your journey to work, how you travel, how far it is and that sort of thing.

MURRAY: Oh... Oh yes of course.

SALLY: Oh good! Well, how do you get to work?

MURRAY: I go by car.

SALLY: By car... Mmm... and how far is it?

MURRAY: It's about seven miles.

SALLY: And how long does it take?

MURRAY: Er... let's see... it usually takes about twenty-five minutes. That's in the rush-hour, of course.

SALLY: Yes . . . and how much does it cost you?

MURRAY: Cost? Nothing! Oh, I see— you mean in petrol?

SALLY: Yes—and in tax and insurance.

MURRAY: Oh, well, about 50p in petrol and about another 50p in tax and insurance, I suppose. About a pound altogether.

SALLY: And how much does it cost by bus, do you know?

MURRAY: By bus? Er... about 50p.

SALLY: Do you ever go by bus?

MURRAY: No, never. I went by bus once and I was an hour late for work.

SALLY: I see. Thank you.

UNIT 18

Set 1

Ask and say how people get to work
Say how you get to work

How do you get to work? I go by car/bus/train
I walk

---

1. Roleplaying
Work with your partner. Look at the chart. One of you answers for
the people at Focus Films, like this:

   How do you get to work, Murray?
I go by car.

How do you get to work, George?
I ....

Name	Murray Freeman	George Blake	Jackie Young	Allan Simmons	Tessa Richards
Method of transport	car	bus	walks	train and bus	car
Distance to work in miles	7	2	$\frac{1}{2}$	8	$5\frac{1}{2}$
Time	25 mins	15 mins	10 mins	45 mins	20 mins
Cost of journey (single)	75p	20p	—	55p	60p

2. Ask your partner how he gets to work/school/college, like this:

   How do you get to work/school/college, ... ?
I ....

How does Murray get to work? He goes by car.

---

3. Ask and answer about the people at Focus Films, like this:

How does Murray get to work?
He goes by car.

How does George get to work?
He ....

4. Ask somebody in the class about their partner, like this:

How does .... get to work/school/college?
He/she ....

Set 2 — Ask and say how often people do things
Say how often you do things

Set 3 — Ask and say how far away places are

Getting to work

MURRAY: always by car – never by bus
GEORGE: usually by bus – sometimes cycles
JACKIE: often walks – sometimes by bus
ALLAN: usually by train and bus – sometimes by car
TESSA: always by car – never by bus

Do you ever go by bus? No, never.

---

1. **Ask the people at Focus about their journeys to work again. Ask and answer like this:**

   Do you ever go by bus, Murray?
   No, never.

   Do you ever cycle, George?
   Yes, sometimes.

2. **Ask your partner if he/she ever goes by car**
   goes by bus
   goes by train
   walks
   cycles

Write down what he/she says. Then tell the class

How does Murray get to work? He always goes by car.

---

3. **Ask and answer about the Focus people like this:**

   How does George get to work?   He usually goes by bus
   but he sometimes cycles.
   How does .... get to work?   He/she ....

4. **Ask your partner like this:**
   How do you get to work...............? I...............(but...............)

5. **Ask about somebody else in the class, like this:**
   How does .... get to work?
   He/she .... (but ....)

Does Murray ever go by car? Yes, always.

---

6. **Ask and answer about the Focus people like this:**
   Does George ever cycle? Yes, Sometimes.
   Does Tessa ever go by bus? No, never.
   Does ....

7. **Ask about somebody else in the class in the same way**

How far is it to work?
It's about seven miles.

½ mile   = half a mile
1 mile   = a mile
1½ miles = one and a half miles
2 miles = two miles
2½ miles = two and a half miles
(5 miles = 8 kilometres)

---

1. **Ask the people at Focus how far it is to work. Work with a partner, like this:**

   How far is it to work, Murray?
   It's about seven miles.

2. **Ask your partner how far it is from his/her house to work/school/college, like this:**
   How far is it to...........?
   It's about ....kilometres/miles.

UNIT 18

Set 4 Ask and say how long journeys take

Set 5 Ask and say how much things cost

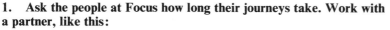

How long does it take? It takes about 25 minutes.

How much does it cost?
It costs about £1 (a pound)

1. **Ask the people at Focus how long their journeys take. Work with a partner, like this:**

How long does it take, Murray?
It takes about twenty-five minutes.

2. **Ask your partner how long his/her journey takes, like this:**

How long does it take, ...?
It takes about ....

Note: 1 hr 10 mins=an hour and ten minutes
1 hr 30 mins=an hour and a half

1. **Ask the people at Focus how much their journeys cost. Work with a partner. Ask and answer like this:**

How much does it cost, Murray?
It costs about £1.

2. **Ask your partner how much his/her journey costs, like this:**

How much does it cost, ...?
It costs about ....

EXTENSION

1. **Listen to Sally Baker interviewing some other people about their journeys to work. Fill in the information in the survey below.**
Then interview somebody in the class and fill in the information in the last column

Name:	David Richards	Martha Hunt	Paul Blake	
Method of transport				
Distance				
Time				
Cost				

2.  i) **This graph shows an average pattern of how people travel to work in Manchester. 200 people were interviewed**

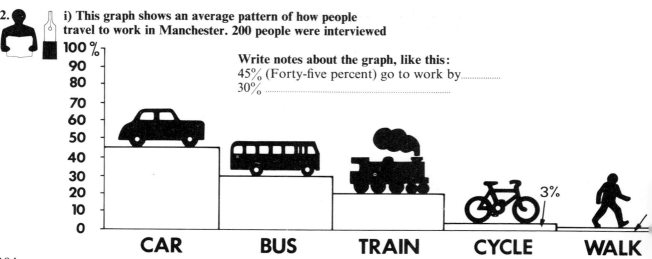

Write notes about the graph, like this:
45% (Forty-five percent) go to work by ....
30% ....

3%

CAR BUS TRAIN CYCLE WALK

ii) This graph shows the time it takes to travel 10 miles by car, train and bus into the city centre.

Write notes on the graph, like this:
It takes .... minutes to travel 10 miles by ....
whereas ....

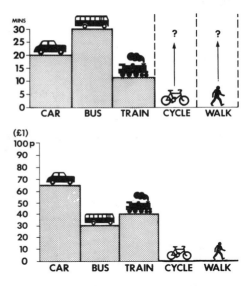

iii) This graph shows the cost of travelling 10 miles by all the methods of transport

Write notes on the graph, like this:
It costs .... to travel 10 miles by ....
However, if you cycle/go by ....

iv) Now write a report about what you have found out about travelling to work in Manchester

3. **You will hear five different people going to work. Listen and write down their method of transport**

1. ....   4. ....
2. ....   5. ....
3. ....

Urgent Press Release from the Citizens' Rights Action Group (CRAG)

Angry parents protested outside the Town Hall in Manchester today about how their children get to school. Mothers had placards saying: BUILD MORE SCHOOLS! STOP SCHOOL BUSES! and one small child had a placard saying: I WANT TO WALK TO SCHOOL! I'M ALWAYS LATE WHEN I GO BY SCHOOL BUS!

The problem is this: there are not enough primary schools in Central Manchester. Small children aged 5-7 travel over five miles to get to school. They go on special school buses. These buses cost Manchester Education Authority £25,000 a year.

The mothers complain that the buses are never on time. The children get up early and sometimes wait half an hour on cold mornings when the bus is late. Then the journey takes a long time in the rush hour in Central Manchester. The children are often late for school, and the teachers are angry.

The mothers also say that sometimes the children do not get home before dark. Sometimes a driver is ill and the bus does not arrive. Then the school telephones the parents. When the children get home they are tired and do not want to do their homework.

CRAG SAYS: SUPPORT THESE PARENTS! JOIN THE CAMPAIGN TO BUILD MORE SCHOOLS!

Citizens' Rights Action Group, 26 Kingscross Avenue, Manchester 5.
Tel: 563 8690

UNIT 18

OPEN DIALOGUE

Talk to Sally about your journey to work, school or college.

SALLY: Hello. Can you answer some questions?
STUDENT: ....
SALLY: They're about your journey to work every day – or to school or college. My first question is: how do you get there – by car, by bicycle, or how?
STUDENT: ....
SALLY: I see. How far is it from your home?
STUDENT: ....
SALLY: Can you tell me how long it takes you?
STUDENT: ....
SALLY: And how much does that cost you?
STUDENT: ....
SALLY: Where do you live? I don't remember.
STUDENT: ....
SALLY: And where do you work or go to school?
STUDENT: ....
SALLY: Oh yes. That's right. Well, thank you. That's very interesting. Oh, one more question – do you always travel this way?
STUDENT: ....
SALLY: I see. Thank you.

ORAL EXERCISES

1. Ask the people at Focus how they get to work. Look at page 102
How do you get to work, Murray? By car?
Yes, that's right.

How do you get to work, George? By bus?
Yes, that's right.

2. Say how you get to work. This time answer for the people at Focus
How do you get to work, Murray?
I go by car.

How do you get to work, George?
I go by bus.

3. Say how people usually get to work. Look at page 103
How does Murray get to work?
He always goes by car.

How does George get to work?
He usually goes by bus.

4. Say how people usually get to work
Does Murray ever go by car?
Yes, he always does.

Does George ever go by bus?
Yes, he usually does.

Does Tessa ever go by bus?
No, she never does.

5. Ask how long it takes people to get to work. Look at page 102 again
Murray lives about 7 miles away.
How long does his journey take if he goes by car?

George lives about 2 miles away.
How long does his journey take if he goes by bus?

6. Talk about the distance and time to get to work Answer for the people at Focus again
How far is it to work, Murray?
It's about 7 miles. It takes about 25 minutes by car.

How far is it to work, George?
It's about 2 miles. It takes about 15 minutes by bus.

REMEMBER

This is how you:

1. Ask and say how people get to work	How do you get to work?
	How does he/she get to work?
	He/she goes by car.
2. Say how you get to work	I go by bus.
	I walk.
3. Ask and say how often people do things	Do you ever go by bus?
	Does he ever walk?
	Yes, always.
	No, never.
	She sometimes goes by bus.
4. Say how often you do things	I usually go by train.
5. Ask and say how far away places are	How far is it?
	It's about 7 miles (kilometres)
6. Ask and say how long journeys take	How long does it take?
	It takes about 25 minutes.
7. Ask and say how much things cost	How much does it cost?
	It costs about £1.

Grammar

How	do	you they	get travel	to	work school? college
	does	he she			

I We They	always usually often	go	by car
He She	sometimes never	goes	

I We They	walk cycle
He She	walks cycles

How long does	it the journey	take (you) (him) (her) ? (them)

It takes (me) (us) (him) (her) (them)	about	an hour 20 minutes

Half	a mile an hour

a mile an hour	and a half

Two Three	and a half	miles hours

Words and Phrases

an article	a minute	always	ask (asked)	how?
	an hour	usually	travel (travelled)	how far?
a journey	a mile	often	get to (got to)	how long?
a tax	a kilometre	sometimes	take (took)	
an insurance		never	cost (cost)	by (by bus)
a rush-hour	a question		walk (walked)	whereas
a bicycle	a percent	about	cycle (cycled)	however
petrol		nothing		
traffic				
an accident		angry		

Focus on people at work

1 Meet Walter Moaney. Walter is an engineer. He works for Ford in a factory in Coventry.

2 Here is a typical day for Walter. He gets up at 7 o'clock and has breakfast.

3 Then he goes to work. He goes to work by bus. He starts work at 8 o'clock.

4 He usually has lunch in the factory canteen.

5 He finishes work at 5.30. Then he goes home and has supper.

6 After supper he usually reads the paper and watches television.

7 He sometimes goes out to the pub and has a pint of beer.

8 He goes to bed at about 10.30.

9 Walter lives in a small house in Coventry. He's married with four children.

10 He and his wife are Irish. They like Coventry but they prefer Ireland. Walter says: "I like my job here but Ireland is my home".

Set 1

Ask what people do every day
Say what people do every day
Say what you do every day

Focus on daily routine

Name & Job	gets up at	starts work at	has lunch	finishes work at	after supper	goes to bed at
Walter Moaney (engineer)	7.00	8.00	in the canteen	5.30	reads the paper and watches TV	about 10.30
Sally Baker (journalist)	7.30	9.00	at work	5.00	goes to see friends or does the housework	about 11.30
David Richards (teacher)	8.00	9.15	at school	4.30	marks homework and reads the paper	about 11.00
Martha Hunt (doctor)	6.30	8.00	in the hospital canteen	4.00	reads, plays records, listens to the radio	about 10.30
Doris Blake (housewife)	7.15	8.00	at home	9.00	watches TV and does the ironing	about 11.00
Paul Blake (student)	8.45	10.00	in the student canteen at college	4.00	studies, or goes to see friends, or goes out for a beer	12.00

1. Ask and answer like this:

➡ a) What time does Walter get up?
He gets up at seven o'clock.

What time does Sally get up?
She gets up at .... etc.

➡ b) What time does Walter start work?
He starts work at eight o'clock.

What time does Sally start work?
She starts work at .... etc.

➡ c) Where does Walter have lunch?
He has lunch in the canteen.

Where does Sally have lunch?
She has lunch .... etc.

d) What time does Walter finish work?
He finishes work at half-past five.

What time does Sally finish work?
She finishes work at .... etc.

e) What does Walter do after supper?
He reads the paper and watches television.

What does Sally do after supper?
She .... etc.

f) What time does Walter go to bed?
He goes to bed at about half-past ten.

What time does Sally go to bed?
She goes to bed at about .... etc.

2. Now ask and answer all the questions about each of the people in turn, like this:

What time does Walter get up?
What time does he start work?
Where does he have lunch?
What time does he finish work?
What does he do after supper?
What time does he go to bed?

3. Here are Murray's notes for the programme about Walter Moaney

```
This is a typical day for
Walter Moaney, an engineer.
He gets up at 7.00 and has
breakfast.  Then he goes to
work.  He starts at 8.00.
He usually has lunch in the
canteen.  He finishes work
at 5.30.  Then he goes
home and has supper.  After
supper he usually reads the
paper and watches T.V.  He
goes to bed at about 10.30.
```

Now write programme notes for
i)   Sally Baker
ii) David Richards
iii) Martha Hunt

4. **Complete the questionnaire about your daily routine**

```
┌─────────────────────────────────────────────┐
│                QUESTIONNAIRE                  │
│ ┌─────────────────────────────────────────┐ │
│ │                                           │ │
│ │ Name:                                     │ │
│ │ _____  │ │
│ │ Address:                                  │ │
│ │ _____  │ │
│ │ Name of School or College                 │ │
│ │    or Institution:                        │ │
│ │ _____  │ │
│ │ Time you get up:                          │ │
│ │ _____  │ │
│ │ Time you start work or                    │ │
│ │    school or college:                     │ │
│ │ _____  │ │
│ │ Time you finish work                      │ │
│ │    or school or college:                  │ │
│ │ _____  │ │
│ │ What you usually do                       │ │
│ │    after supper:                          │ │
│ │ _____  │ │
│ │ Time you go to bed:                       │ │
│ │                                           │ │
│ └─────────────────────────────────────────┘ │
└─────────────────────────────────────────────┘
```

5. **Now ask your partner about his/her typical day, like this:**

    What time do you get up? I get up at ....
        What time do you start work (school or college)?
        What time do you finish work (school or college)?
        What do you usually do after supper?
        What time do you go to bed?

        Make notes on what your partner says

6. **Now tell the class about your partner's daily routine, like this:**

        He/she gets up at .... He/she starts work at
        ....

7. **Group Activity**
 i) **Find out the time most people get up**
                        start school or work or college
                        finish school or work or college
                        go to bed
ii) **Find out what most people do after supper**

8. **Now write a few lines about your group. Write like this:**

DAILY ROUTINE - REPORT

In our group most people get up at..........
They start ....

UNIT 19

Ask people about their jobs
Say who people work for and where they work
Say who you work for and where you work

What does Walter do? He's an engineer.
He works for Ford.
He works in a car factory in Coventry.

Name	Job	Company/Authority	Place of work
Walter Moaney	an engineer	Ford	car factory in Coventry
David Richards	a teacher	Manchester Council	school outside Manchester
Martha Hunt	a doctor	National Health Service	hospital in Manchester
Sally Baker	a journalist	The Manchester News	office in the centre of Manchester
Doris Blake	a housewife		at home
George Blake	a technician	Focus Films	studio at the Focus Film Centre

1. **Ask and answer like this:**

    What does David do? He's a ....
    He works for ....
    He works in a ....

2. **Now ask your partner what he/she does, like this:**

    What do you do?
    I'm a/an..................................
    (I work for ....)
    I (work in a/an..................................)
    (study at ....)

EXTENSION

1. Listen to the interview with Walter Moaney and follow the pictures and text on page 108

2.

ring and should not
included. There is
class-consciousness
nd and the gaunt
R. Leavis looms
rge.

John
.ntribu-
cial iso-
. Read at
or Bron,
ary, is the
ither book
e to tackle
bridge con-
i-on:

.ied for years to
eling that Oxford
oridge types are
nd very different
is not easy to sub-
. The very colours
suggest them, the
k blue and the pale
lue, the highly poli-
rld of Oxford social
nd savoir-faire, the
ritan, inward, Arts
nce Cambridge of
and simple, with
bursts of self-
'ity. Even the
reinforce
Oxford
ningled in
nd the de-
real life;
flat lands,
parate, im-
sible, ob-
tarty and
iris, where
ondon, is
mixed, harder
ichly repaying

very truthful
am basically
d read English
consequences
nink I should
fared better at
ere I had a
anuel, which
ted.

hand, I was
rd as were
early all the
to My Ox-
deal happier
bridge con-
the present
I believe to
erience but
and these
ear it out,
a better
real and

their undergraduate days and
to set it all down unflinch-
ingly and con brio is no
mean achievement and Ms
Thwaite has pulled it off. I
was not able to detect a
single example of slack writing in her collection; Mr
Hayman's, alas, contains two
or three contributions that
might better have been con-
signed to oblivion.
The Oxford book is a
masterpiece of its kind, al-
though, if one wanted to be

Thatcher, another contem-
porary; Antonia Fraser, in a
well sustained piece, sees it
all in terms of clothes and in
some ways she is right: "At
at Oxford, in academic dress,
I succeeded in what I suppose had always been my
aim: looking exactly like
everybody else"; Alan Coren,
in what is, predictably,
the funniest piece, woman-
izes in digs on the Iffley
Road; Martin Amis did
so less successfully; in fact,

rather be
have been.
too much
flying arou.
figure of F.
unnecessarily la.

I identified wit..
Vaisey's sensitive co
tion and with the so
lation of Piers Paul
St John's. Elean
another contempor
only writer in e
with the courag
the Oxford/Cam
frontation head

"I have tr.
justify a fe
and Camb
distinct a
though it
stantiate
seem to
rich dar
ascetic b
tical wo.
veneer
chill, pu
and Scie.
savoir pure.
occasional a
conscious frivo..
physical settings
these images,
warmer, lusher, r
with the town a
caying fumes of
Cambridge in the.
bleak, spartan, se
mediately acces-
viously pretty,
heartless like Pa
Oxford, like I
grander, more I
to know but r.
exploration."

I find this
and since I
puritanical an
with disastrous
at Oxford, I tl
probably have f

FACE TO FACE

This week with *Barry Miles* from the Royal Exchange Theatre.

Barry Miles is an actor from the Royal Exchange Theatre in Manchester. Just now you can see him in Shakespeare's 'Othello' where he plays the leading role.

Our reporter, Sally Baker, asked him about his typical day. He says: "I get up at ten, have breakfast - orange juice, an egg and a cup of black coffee - and read the paper. Then at eleven I go to the theatre and rehearse. Not Othello but our next production. Then what? A late lunch at the pub with the others. Then we're free in the afternoon. Sometimes I go to the cinema, go shopping or see friends. Tea at five, then I go back to the theatre. The evening performance starts at seven thirty. After the performance? We all go to the theatre bar, have drinks and talk. I usually have some sandwiches then. I go to bed late, about one o'clock. Yes, that's quite a typical day for me".

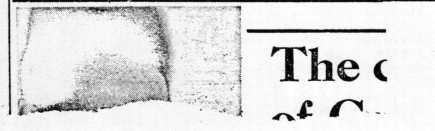

The (
of C

Now write an article for the Manchester News and say what Barry did yesterday

'Air

UNIT 19

OPEN DIALOGUE

Talk to Sally about what you do every day

SALLY: Hello! Well, as you know, I'm a journalist for the Manchester News. What do you do?

STUDENT: ....

SALLY: Oh, yes... where?

STUDENT: ....

SALLY: What time do you get up in the morning?

STUDENT: ....

SALLY: And go to bed?

STUDENT: ....

SALLY: That's a long day. What do you usually do after supper?

STUDENT: ....

SALLY: Oh, do you? I usually go out and see friends. Well, I must go back to the office now. Bye!

STUDENT: ....

ORAL EXERCISES

1. Ask where people work
Walter's an engineer.
Oh, yes. Where does he work?

Jackie's a secretary.
Oh, yes. Where does she work?

2. Say what people do every day. Look at page 109
What time does Walter get up?
He gets up at seven.

And what time does he start work?
He starts work at eight.

What time does Sally get up?
She gets up at seven-thirty.

3. Say what you do every day. You are Doris Blake. Look at page 109
What time do you get up, Doris?
I get up at quarter past seven.

And what time do you start work round the house.
I start work at eight o'clock.

4. Ask what people do every day. Look at page 109 again. Ask about Walter
What time does he get up?
At seven.

What time does he start work?
At eight.

5. Ask what people do every day. Look at page 109. Ask Sally
What time do you get up, Sally?
I get up at seven-thirty.

What time do you start work?
I start work at nine.

6. Answer the questions. Look at page 109.
Does Walter have lunch in the canteen?
Yes, that's right, he does.

Does he finish work at six?
No, he doesn't. He finishes work at half-past five.

REMEMBER

This is how you:

1.	Ask what people do every day	What time do you get up?
		What time does he go to bed?
2.	Say what people do every day	He gets up at 7.00.
		He has lunch at work.
3.	Say what you do every day	I get up at 8.00.
		After supper I watch T.V.
4.	Ask people about their jobs	What do you do?
		What does he do?
5.	Say who people work for and where they work	He works for Ford. He works in a car factory in Coventry.
6.	Say who you work for and where you work	I work for Focus Films.
		I work in a studio in Focus Film Centre.

Grammar

What time	do	you	get up?
			start work?
	does	he	finish work?
		she	go to bed?

I	get up	at	7.00
He	gets up		9.00
She	starts work		

Where	do	you	have lunch?
	does	he	
		she	

I	usually	have lunch	in the canteen
He			
She	sometimes	has lunch	

Where	do	you	work?
	does	he	
		she	

I	work	in an office in Manchester
He		
She	works	

What	do	you	do after supper?
	does	he	
		she	

I	watch	television
He		
She	watches	

Words and Phrases

a factory	breakfast	get up (got up)	read (read) the paper (newspaper)
a canteen		go to work	do (did) the housework
a hospital	at work	go to bed	do the ironing
a studio	at school	go home	mark (marked) homework
a radio	at college	have (had) (breakfast etc.)	study (studied)
a pub		work for (worked)	listen to (listened to) (the radio)
a pint		prefer (preferred)	play (played) (records)
a wife	early		
a husband			

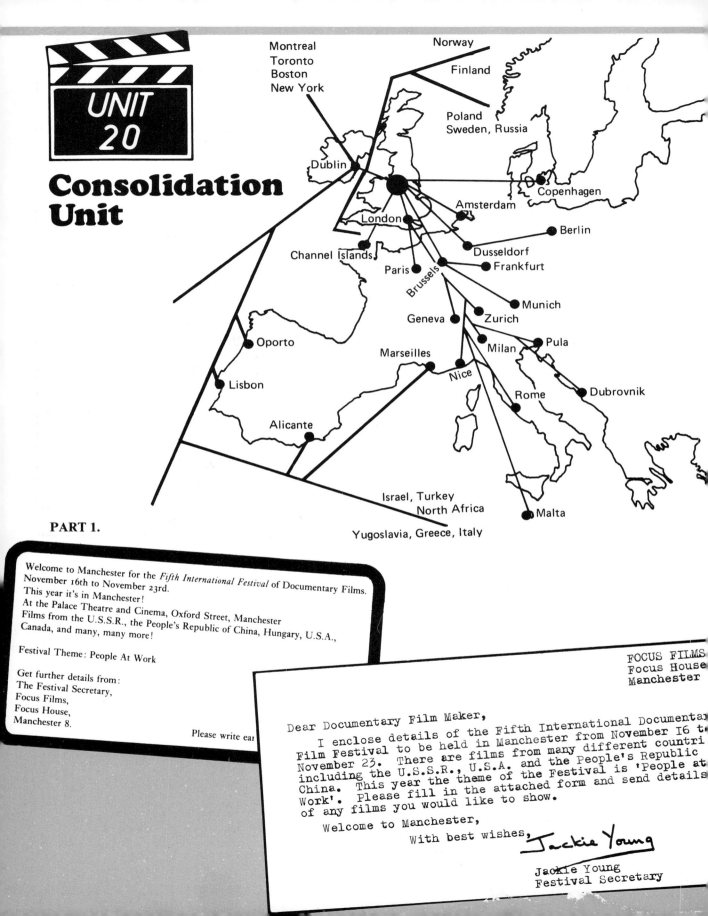

UNIT 20

Consolidation Unit

PART 1.

Welcome to Manchester for the *Fifth International Festival* of Documentary Films.
November 16th to November 23rd.
This year it's in Manchester!
At the Palace Theatre and Cinema, Oxford Street, Manchester
Films from the U.S.S.R., the People's Republic of China, Hungary, U.S.A.,
Canada, and many, many more!

Festival Theme: People At Work

Get further details from:
The Festival Secretary,
Focus Films,
Focus House,
Manchester 8.

Please write ear

FOCUS FILMS
Focus House
Manchester

Dear Documentary Film Maker,
    I enclose details of the Fifth International Documentar
Film Festival to be held in Manchester from November 16 t
November 23. There are films from many different countri
including the U.S.S.R., U.S.A. and the People's Republic
China. This year the theme of the Festival is 'People at
Work'. Please fill in the attached form and send details
of any films you would like to show.

    Welcome to Manchester,

        With best wishes, *Jackie Young*

                Jackie Young
                Festival Secretary

Festival Administration Office—Manchester Airport
Please fill in this form to help make your stay in Manchester a pleasant one.

Name	Mizuki Brown	Buzz Anderson	Gina Colbert	
Nationality	American	Australian	French	
Domicile	San Francisco	Sydney	Montreal	
Occupation	Journalist	Cameraman	Student. at University	
Professional Interests	the history of the cinema	underwater photography	films about ordinary people.	
Personal Interests	modern art, photography	sport, stamps	reading, music, foreign languages	
Type of Accommodation required	Hotel (full board)	Guest House (bed and breakfast)	Hostel (bed and breakfast)	
Food/drink	Vegetarian	I like everything	I don't drink or smoke	
Other interests while in Manchester	I would like to visit the Manchester News office	I would like to see a football match with Manchester United.	I would like to see Manchester University	
Signed	Mizuki Brown	Buzz Anderson	Gina Colbert	

A reporter from Manchester Radio interviews Mizuki Brown

JOHN MENZIES:	Hello, my name is John Menzies. I am a reporter for Manchester Radio. You are a visitor to the Fifth International Festival of Documentary Films?
MIZUKI:	That's right.
JOHN MENZIES:	May I ask you some questions?
MIZUKI:	Yes, of course.
JOHN MENZIES:	Your name is ....?
MIZUKI:	Mizuki Brown.
JOHN MENZIES:	And what nationality are you, Mizuki?
MIZUKI:	American.
JOHN MENZIES:	Where in the U.S.A. are you from, Mizuki?
MIZUKI:	I'm from San Francisco.
JOHN MENZIES:	And, what do you do?
MIZUKI:	I'm a journalist.
JOHN MENZIES:	What are your professional interests, Mizuki?
MIZUKI:	I'm interested in the history of the camera.
JOHN MENZIES:	And your personal interests?
MIZUKI:	Modern art and photography.

UNIT 20

JOHN MENZIES: I see. And where are you staying in Manchester?
MIZUKI: In a hotel.
JOHN MENZIES: Finally, what would you like to do or see in
Manchester – apart from the Film Festival?
MIZUKI: Oh, I would like to visit the Manchester News office.
JOHN MENZIES: Thank you very much.

1. **Work with a partner. Interview Buzz Anderson and Gina
   Colbert.**
2. **Fill in your own name and personal information in the empty
   column on page 117. Your professional interests can be about
   anything, not necessarily films or photography.**
3. **Interview your partner as in Exercise 1.**

4. ◖◗ **Listen to the conversation between Mizuki Brown and Buzz
   Anderson when they meet for the first time. They meet in the
   Festival Theatre before the first film.**

5. **Roleplaying**
**You go to Manchester for the festival. You meet another visitor.
Act out the conversation, like the one between Mizuki and Buzz,
and remember to do the following:**

Introduce yourself
Say where you are from
Say what you do (what your job is)
Offer the other person a drink
Offer him/her a cigarette
Ask about his/her interests
Say what your interests are
Suggest that you go into the theatre to get a good seat.

The date is
November 16th
The place is
The Palace Theatre Manchester
The event is
The Fifth International Festival of Documentary Films

6. Murray Freeman, film director from Focus Films of Manchester, opened the
   festival with the following speech:

"Good evening, Ladies and Gentlemen. It is my great pleasure, this evening, to
open the Fifth International Festival of Documentary Films. Many of you were at
the festival last year in Munich. The theme then was 'How People Live'. We had
entries from all over the world. We saw some very interesting and professional
films and we all learnt a lot about how people live in different countries. This year
the theme is 'People at Work' and I am sure that, once again, the festival will be
a rewarding experience for all of us.

As one of the film directors at Focus Films, I would like to introduce our own
entry for the festival: 'Focus on People at Work'. To make the film, we went to
Newcastle, to Coventry, to London and to Bristol. We interviewed a policeman,
an engineer, a secretary and a housewife. We went to a police-station, a car factory,
a busy London office and an ordinary home. We saw people at work, we saw people
in their homes. We saw a lot that was depressing but we did our best to give a
balanced picture of the ordinary British worker. We hope that the film will be both
interesting and informative. Ladies and gentlemen, may I present the first film,
a Focus Film Production: 'Focus on People at Work'."

WHAT is the link between
Phileas Fogg here of 'Around the | hands, has remained fundam

PART 2

1. Put these activities in the right order of time.

go to work
have supper
get up
go home
watch television
have lunch
go to bed
have breakfast
finish work

2. Write the opposite meaning of these words

e.g. single .... return (ticket)

get up ....

start ....

open ....

always ....

beautiful (weather) ....

leave (train) ....

morning ....

black ....

3. Put these words into groups of three

afternoon	door	interesting	usually
lunch	often	suitcase	bus
sometimes	letter	factory	supper
window	morning	envelope	hospital
car	office	breakfast	beautiful
evening	lovely	train	stamp

4. Say these times from a time table

e.g. 16.35 ...Twenty-five to five.

7.45	23.55	14.25
16.40	6.30	7.15
10.20	15.35	12.00
	11.05	

5. Fill in the correct prepositions in the gaps. Choose from these:

on   at   in   to   by

1. The train arrives .... six o'clock.
2. Are you free .... Saturday evening.
3. His birthday is .... Tuesday.
4. The film starts .... five thirty .... the evening.
5. I go .... work .... car.
6. Can you meet me .... the station?
7. He lives .... Manchester.
8. My birthday is .... December 23rd.
9. The film is .... the Plaza cinema.
10. She has lunch .... home.
11. He goes .... college every day.
12. He has lunch .... the canteen .... work.

6. Fill in the correct form of the verbs in brackets

1. He .... in an office in Manchester. (work)
2. .... he .... in Manchester too? (live)
3. Where .... they .... (live)?
4. He .... work at eight o'clock. (start)
5. We .... work at six o'clock. (finish)
6. When .... you .... lunch? (have)
7. She .... breakfast at seven o'clock. (have)
8. How long .... the journey ....? (take)
9. When .... she...............? (go to bed)
10. It .... about half an hour. (take)
11. He usually .... television after supper. (watch)
12. It .... about 40p. (cost)

7. Fill in the correct personal pronoun in the gaps. Choose between:

me   you   him   her   us   them

Example: He's busy just now. Can you ring him this evening?

1. I'm busy just now. Can you ring .... tomorrow?
2. I'm afraid she isn't here. Can you ring .... this afternoon?
3. They're at the station. Can you meet ....?
4. We're busy just now. Can you ask .... next week?
5. He isn't at home. Can you ring .... tomorrow?
6. If you're busy now, can I see .... tomorrow?
7. My train arrives at six p.m. Can you meet .... at the station?
8. They're in London today. Ask .... on Monday.

8. Fill in the correct form of the verb in the past tense. Use the verb in brackets

1. I (go) to the theatre on Saturday night.
2. What (you see)?
3. Where (he go) last night?
4. I (see) an old Hitchcock film.
5. What (she have) to eat?
6. She (have) a sandwich and a cup of coffee.
7. What (you do) yesterday?
8. I (do) the washing and the garden.

9. Fill in the gaps in these dialogues

1. **(At the station)**

   A: ....
   B: The train to London? It leaves at 8.15.
   A: ....
   B: Platform 5.

2. **(At home)**

   A: ....
   B: Yes, of course. What can I get you?
   A: ....
   B: Milk and bread. All right.

3. A: Hello! Where are you?
   B: ....
   A: The station?
   B: ....
   A: Yes, of course.
      I'll come in my car.
      I'll be there at 4 o'clock.

4. MARIA: 477 9372. Hello?
   JOE: ....
   MARIA: Oh, hello Joe. How are you?
   JOE: ....
   MARIA: Oh, I'm all right.
   JOE: ....
   MARIA: Tonight? Yes, I'd love to. What film is it?
   JOE: ....
   MARIA: Oh yes, I'd like to see 'The Carlton Affair'. What time does it start?
   JOE: ....
   MARIA: Half-past seven? All right but where shall we meet?
   JOE: ....
   MARIA: All right. You know my address, don't you?
   JOE: ....
   MARIA: Yes. Goodbye.

5. A: ....
   B: Oh, usually quite late. About half past seven or eight o'clock.
   A: ....
   B: At nine o'clock. I'm a teacher, you see.
   A: ....
   B: In a school outside Manchester.
   A: ....
   B: At school. In the school canteen. The lunches are quite good.

6. A: ....
   B: By car.
   A: ....
   B: No, never. I don't like buses.
   A: ....
   B: Oh, about five miles.
   A: ....
   B: To get to work? About twenty minutes in the rush-hour.

7. A: What's the matter?
   B: ....
   A: Bored? Well, what do you want to do?
   B: ....
   A: Oh no, not the club. Let's go to the cinema.

8. A: ....
   B: Yes thanks, a very nice evening.
   A: ....
   B: I went to the cinema.
   A: ....
   B: An old Hitchcock film.

INFORMATION SHEET

MANCHESTER

is a major centre of commerce and industry. The ease of communication with other commercial and industrial centres abroad is illustrated by the flying times from Manchester International Airport to the following destinations:

Destination	Distance (miles)	Time (hrs/mins)
Amsterdam	312	1.05
Berlin (via Dusseldorf)	712	2.50
Brussels	335	1.05
Copenhagen	624	1.40
Dusseldorf	403	1.15
Geneva	585	1.40
Malta	1459	4.00
Milan	754	3.00
Montreal (via Prestwick)	3199	7.50
Munich	708	1.55
New York	3332	7.30
Paris	366	1.15
Toronto (via Montreal)	3500	8.40
Zurich	627	1.50

the diligent research and enthusiasm of the author.

And Mr Heath spoke of the tremendous help he had received from everybody, including complete strangers

edition are opening.

The book will be sim to the other seven wh Barracuda Books has duced for Hertfords communities.

FOCUS SURVEY ON LEISURE ACTIVITIES

300 people over the age of 30 were asked what they usually do in the evening after supper. The following figures were obtained:

65% watch TV and read the paper (70% of these watch TV only)

15% do housework

12% go out (to the cinema, to see friends, to the pub etc)

5% listen to the radio, play records or read a book

3% work or study

10. Work with a partner. Ask and answer questions like this:

How long does it take to fly from Manchester to Amsterdam?
It takes one hour five minutes.

How long does it take to fly to Berlin?
It takes two hours fifty minutes.

11. In England it is clear that most people watch television in the evening. What about your country? What do most people do in the evening in your country? Discuss in groups.

Words and Phrases

a language	foreign	fly
the world		
art	abroad	
photography		

HOW TO SAY IT

	Function	Example Sentence	Unit : Set
Accept	Accept something	*Yes please.*	10:1
	Accept apologies	*That's all right!*	11
	Accept invitations to do things	*Yes, I'd love to.*	17:3
Address	Spell your address		4
Agree	Agree to do something	*Yes, of course.*	14:1
		Yes, OK.	
	Agree with suggestions	*Yes, that's a good idea!*	15:2
Answer	Answer the telephone	*872 4679. Hello?*	17:1
		Yes, speaking.	
Apologise	Apologise	*Sorry!*	11
	Accept apologies	*That's all right!*	11
Arrange	Arrange to meet somebody	*Are you free tomorrow evening?*	17:2
		Yes, I am/No, I'm afraid I'm not.	
Ask for	Ask for things	*Can I have a biscuit, please?*	10:2
Attention	Attract attention	*Excuse me!*	1
Can	Say you can't do things	*I'm sorry, I can't (just now).*	14:1
Conversation	Start a conversation	*How are you?*	17:1
		Fine, thanks! And you?	
		Not too bad.	
Cost	Ask and talk about cost	*How much is it? It's £14.*	9:3
	Ask and say how much things cost	*How much does it cost?*	18:5
Count	Count to twenty		9
Date	Ask about dates	*When's Tessa's birthday?*	15:1
	Talk about dates	*It's on January 10th.*	15:1
		It's on Monday.	
		January 10th is a Monday.	
Disagree	Disagree with suggestions	*No, not flowers.*	15:2
Disappointed	Say you are disappointed	*Oh, what a pity!*	17:2
Dissatisfaction	Express dissatisfaction	*Oh! It isn't very big.*	9:2
Do	Ask people to do things	*Can you buy some fruit?*	14:1
		Can you open the window?	
		Can you meet me at the station?	
	Agree to do something	*Yes, of course.*	14:1
		Yes, OK.	
	Say you can't do things	*I'm sorry, I can't (just now).*	14:1
	Ask people want they want to do	*What do you want to do?*	16:1
	Say what you want to do	*I want to go to the cinema.*	16:1
	Invite people to do things	*Would you like to go to the cinema?*	17:3
	Accept invitations to do things	*Yes, I'd love to.*	17:3
	Refuse invitations to do things	*Sorry, I'm afraid I can't.*	17:3
Far away	Ask and say how far away places are	*How far is it?*	18:3
		It's about seven miles.	
Formal	Thank formally	*Thank you.*	1
	Greet formally	*How do you do!*	2:1
	Say goodbye formally	*Goodbye!*	5
	Accept something	*Yes, please.*	10:1
From	Ask and say where people are from	*Where are you from?*	7:3
		I'm from Melbourne.	
Get	Ask and say how people get to work	*How do you get to work?*	18:1
		How does he/she get to work?	
		He/She goes by car.	
	Say how you get to work	*I go by bus.*	18:1
Give	Ask for and give things	*Can I have a biscuit, please?*	10:2
		Yes, here you are.	
Goodbye	Say goodbye	*Goodbye!*	3
	Say goodbye formally	*Goodbye!*	5
	Make parting remarks	*Bye! See you later.*	17
Greet	Greet formally	*How do you do!*	2:1
	Greet informally	*Hello!*	3:1
	Greet somebody in the morning	*Good morning!*	4

How (see Far away, Get, Long, Much, Often).

Informal	Greet informally	*Hello!*	3:1
	Thank people informally	*Thanks!*	14
Information	Ask for and give specific information	*Which one/ones would you like?*	14:3
		This one./That one over there.	
		These ones./Those ones over there.	
Introduction	Introduce yourself	*My name's Sally Baker.*	2:1
		I'm Sally Baker.	
	Introduce people	*Neville, this is Sally.*	3:1
		Jackie, meet Allan. He's a van driver.	7:1
Invite	Invite people to do things	*Would you like to go to the cinema?*	17:3
	Accept invitations to do things	*Yes, I'd love to.*	17:3
	Refuse invitations to do things	*Sorry, I'm afraid I can't.*	17:3
Job	Ask what somebody's job is	*What do you do?*	2:2
		What does Murray/he do?	
		Is he a film director?	
	Say what your job is	*I'm a journalist.*	2:2
		Sally's a journalist.	3:1
	Ask people about their jobs	*What do you do?/What does she do?*	19:2
Journey	Ask and say how long journeys take	*How long does it take?*	18:4
		It takes about 25 minutes.	
Leave	Say you must leave	*I must go!*	7
Like	Ask what people like	*Do you like tea with lemon?*	11:2
		Does he like tea with lemon?	11:3
	Say what you like	*Yes, I do/No, I don't.*	11:2
		It's all right.	
	Say what other people like	*Yes, he does./No, he doesn't.*	11:3
		He thinks it's all right.	
	Ask what people would like	*What would you like?*	14:2
	Say what you would like	*I'd like some fish/oranges, please.*	14:2
Long	Ask and say how long journeys take	*How long does it take?*	18:4
		It takes about 25 minutes.	
Marital status	Ask and talk about marital status	*Are you married?*	4:1
		Is he/she married?	
		Yes, I am./No, I'm not.	
		Yes, he/she is.	
		No, he/she isn't.	
Meet	Arrange to meet somebody	*Are you free tomorrow evening?*	17:2
		Yes, I am.	
		No, I'm afraid I'm not.	
Much	Ask and say how much things cost	*How much does it cost?*	18:5
		It costs about £1.	
Must	Say you must leave	*I must go!*	7
Name	Ask somebody's name	*What's your name?*	1:1
		What's his/her name?	3:3
	Say your name	*(Sally Baker.)*	1:1
	Say somebody's name	*His/her name's . . .*	3:3
	Spell your name		4:2
	Say your name on the telephone	*It's Allan here.*	17:1
	Introduce yourself	*My name's Sally Baker.*	2:1
Nationality	Ask and talk about nationality	*Are you English?*	7:2
		Yes, I am/No, I'm not. I'm Australian.	
Number	Say your telephone number		4:3
Often	Ask and say how often people do things	*Do you ever go by bus?*	18:2
		Does he ever walk?	
		Yes, always./No, never.	
		She sometimes goes by train.	
	Say how often you do things	*I usually go by train.*	18:2
Offer	Offer something	*Would you like a cup of tea?*	10:1
Part	Make parting remarks	*Bye! See you later.*	17
Past	Ask about the past	*Where were you yesterday?*	16:2
		What did you do yesterday?	
		Where did you go?	
		What did you see?	
	Talk about the past	*I was at home.*	16:2
		I went to London.	
		I did the washing.	

124

I saw 'The Carlton Affair'.
I had a cup of coffee.
It was quite good.

People (see Do, Introduce, Invite, Job, Like, Live, Often, Thank, Where, Work)

Places	Ask where places are	*Where's Kent Road?*	1:2
	Say where places are	*It's over there.*	1:2
		It's next to the station.	5:1
	Show and ask about places	*This is the kitchen.*	9:1
		Is this the kitchen?	
		Yes, it is/No, it isn't.	
	Ask and say how far away places are	*How far is it?*	18:3
		It's about seven miles.	
Pleased	Express pleasure	*What a lovely room!*	15:3
		What beautiful flowers!	
	Say you are pleased	*Oh, good!*	17
Refuse	Refuse invitations to do things	*Sorry, I'm afraid I can't.*	17:3
Satisfaction	Express satisfaction	*Mmm! It's nice and big.*	9:2
Show	Show and ask about places	*This is the kitchen and that's the bedroom.*	9:1
		Is this the kitchen?	
Spell	Spell your address		4
	Spell your name		4:2
Suggestions	Ask for suggestions	*What shall we give her?*	15:2
		What shall we do?	
	Make suggestions	*Let's give her some flowers.*	15:2
		Let's go to the cinema.	
	Agree with suggestions	*Yes, that's a good idea!*	15:2
	Disagree with suggestions	*No, not flowers!*	15:2
Telephone	Say your telephone number		4:3
	Answer the telephone	*872 4679. Hello?*	17:1
		Yes, speaking.	
	Say your name on the telephone	*It's Allan here.*	17:1
Thank	Thank formally	*Thank you.*	1
	Thank somebody	*Thank you very much.*	3
	Thank informally	*Thanks!*	14
	Thank people for things	*Thank you for the beautiful flowers.*	15
Time	Ask the time	*What's the time?*	11:1
	Say the time	*It's two o'clock.*	11:1
		It's half past two.	
		It's quarter past/to two.	
		It's ten past three.	13:1
		It's five to four.	
	Ask what time things happen	*What time does the train leave?*	13:2
	Say what time things happen	*It leaves at five past nine.*	
		It arrives at six o'clock in the morning.	
Want	Ask people what they want to do	*What do you want to do?*	16:1
	Say what you want to do	*I want to go to the cinema.*	16:1
Weather	Make remarks about the weather	*Lovely day, isn't it?*	14:4
		Yes, beautiful.	

What (see Do, Job, Like, Time).

Where (see Places, Live, Work).

Work	Ask and say how people get to work	*How do you get to work?*	18:1
		How does he/she get to work?	
		He/she goes by car.	
	Say how you get to work	*I go by bus.*	18:1
	Say who people work for and where they work	*He works for Ford. He works in a car factory in Coventry.*	19:2
	Say who you work for and where you work	*I work for Focus Films. I work in a studio in Focus Film Centre.*	

GRAMMAR REVIEW

UNIT 1. Set 1

What's	your name?	(Sally Baker.)
What is		

Set 2

Where's	Kent Road?	It's (It is)	over there.
Where is	Mr Freeman?	He's (He is)	
	Mrs Richards?	She's (She is)	

UNIT 2. Set 1

My name's (name is)	Sally Baker.
I'm	Murray Freeman.

Set 2

What	do	you	do?	I'm (I am)	a	film director.
	does	Murray Tessa		He's (He is) She's (She is)		journalist.

UNIT 3. Set 1

This is	(Sally Baker.)	Sally's (Sally is)	a journalist.
	(Walter Moaney)	Walter's (Walter is)	an engineer.

Set 2

Is	Neville he	a film director?	Yes,	he	is.
	she		No,	she	isn't (is not).

He	isn't	a film director.
She		an engineer

What does	he	do?
	she	

What's (What is)	his	name?	His	name's . . . . . .
	her		Her	

UNIT 4. Set 1

Are	you	married?	Yes,	I am.	No,	I'm not.
Is	he			he		he
	she			she is.		she isn't.

UNIT 5. Set 1

Where's the	bank? post office? cinema?	It's	next to behind in front of opposite near	the	station. park. hotel.

UNIT 7. Set 2

Are	you they	English?
Is	he she	from	England? London?

Yes,	I am.			No,	I'm not.	I'm	
	we	are.			we	aren't.	We're	American.
	they				they		They're	
	he	is.			he	isn't.	He's	from	America.
	she				she		She's		New York.

Look at	my your his her our their	car!

Set 3.

Where	are	you	from?	I'm	from	Liverpool Manchester.
	is	he		He's		Australia.
		she		She's		

UNIT 8. Set 1 and 2

Where do	you	live?
	they	

I	live in		London.
			England.
We		the	north	of England.
			south	
		a suburb of	London.
			Manchester.
They		a suburb	north	of	London.
			south		Manchester.

UNIT 9. Set 1

This is	the	bedroom.
That's		bathroom.
		kitchen.

Is	this	the	bedroom?	Yes, it is.
	that		bathroom?	No, it isn't.
			kitchen?	

Set 2

It's nice and	big. hot. cold.

It isn't very	big. hot. cold.

Set 3

How much is it?	It's	£13 £1 £20	a week.

126

UNIT 10. Set 1

Would you like a	cup of	tea? coffee?
	glass of milk?	
	biscuit?	

Set 2

Can I have a	cup of	tea? coffee?
	glass of milk?	
	biscuit?	

one	cup glass sandwich	two	cups glasses sandwiches

UNIT 11. Set 2 and 3

Do	you	like	tea with lemon? Frank Sinatra? Elizabeth Taylor? small dogs?
Does	he she		

Yes,	I do. he she	does.	No,	I don't. he she	doesn't.

He She	thinks	it's he's she's they're	all right.

UNIT 13. Set 2

What time does	the film it	start?
	the bank it	open?
	the bus it	arrive?

It	starts opens arrives	at	7.15. ten past nine.

It arrives at	4 o'clock	in the	morning. afternoon.
	8 o'clock		morning. evening.

UNIT 14. Set 1

Can you	buy some	fruit? bread? stamps?
	meet	me? him? her? us? them?
	open close	the window? it?

Set 2

I'd like (I would like) some	fruit. bread. stamps.

How many	apples oranges	would you like?

Set 3

Which	one	do you mean?	This That	one.
	ones		These Those	ones.

Set 4

Lovely Beautiful Awful Terrible	day, isn't it?

UNIT 15. Set 1

When's (When is)	your Tessa's	birthday?
	your next	English lesson?

It's on	Monday. Tuesday (etc.) January 10th. November 14th.

Set 2

What shall we	give	her? him? them?
	do?	

Let's (Let us)	give	her him them	a book. some chocolates.
	go to the cinema. have a party.		

What	a	beautiful lovely	film! book!
	an	interesting	

What	beautiful lovely	glasses! people!
	interesting	

UNIT 16. Set 1

What	do	you they	want to do?
	does	he she	

I We They	want	to	go home. invite some friends to dinner.
He She	wants		

Set 2

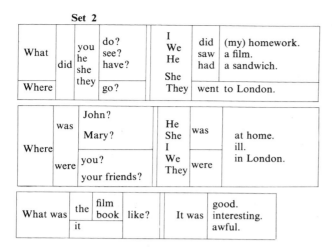

What	did	you / he / she / they	do? / see? / have?	I / We / He / She	did / saw / had	(my) homework. / a film. / a sandwich.
Where			go?	They		went to London.

Where	was	John? / Mary?	He / She / I	was	at home. / ill. / in London.
	were	you? / your friends?	We / They	were	

What was	the (it)	film / book	like?	It was	good. / interesting. / awful.

It takes	(me) / (us) / (him) / (her) / (them)	about	an hour. / 20 minutes.

half	a mile / an hour	a mile / an hour	and a half

two / three (etc.)	and a half	miles. / hours.

UNIT 17. Set 2

On	Monday / Tuesday / Wednesday etc.	morning / afternoon / evening
This / Tomorrow		

Would you like to	go	to the	cinema? / theatre?	I'd love to. (I would)
		out for a	meal? / drink? / walk?	
	come to		lunch? / dinner?	

UNIT 18. Set 1

How	do	you / they	get / travel	to	work? / school? / college?
	does	he / she			

I / We / They	go		car. / bus. / train. / plane. / bicycle.
He / She	goes	by	

Set 2

I / We / They	always / usually / often / sometimes / never	go	by car.	I / We / They	walk. / cycle.
He / She		goes		He / She	walks. / cycles.

Set 4

How long does	it / the journey	take	(you)? / (him)? / (her? / (them)?

UNIT 19. Set 1

What time	do	you	get up? / start work? / finish work? / go to bed?
	does	he / she	

I / He / She	get up / start work (etc.) / gets up / starts work (etc.)	at	7.00. / 9.00.

Where	do	you	have lunch?
	does	he / she	

I / He / She	usually / sometimes	have / has	lunch in the canteen.

What	do	you	do after supper?	I / He / She	watch / watches	television.
	does	he / she				

Set 2

Where	do	you	work?	I / He / She	work / works	in an office in Manchester.
	does	he / she				

WORD LIST

The number in **bold** print beside each word tells you in which Unit the word first appears for you to learn it.

v indicates a *verb*

A
about **18**
abroad **19**
accident **18**
address **4**
after **17**
afternoon **13**
aftershave **15**
again **12**
airport **6**
air terminal **6**
all right! **14**
all right (he's . . .) **11**
also **15**
always **18**
a.m. **13**
America **7**
American **7**
and **3**
angry **18**
answer *v* **11**
apple **14**
April **15**
arrive *v* **13**
art **20**
article **18**
ask *v* **11**
at **14**
at home **15**
August **15**
Australia **7**
Australian **7**
awful **14**

B
bank **5**
bar **6**
bathroom **9**
beach **9**
beautiful **14**
bed **19**
bedroom **4**
beer **10**
before **17**
behind **5**
bicycle **18**
big **9**
birthday **15**
biscuit **10**
black (black coffee) **11**
book **15**
bored **16**
bottle **14**
boy **7**
bread **14**
breakfast **19**
Brighton **8**
bring (brought) *v* **17**
Bristol **8**
brother **7**

bus **6**
but **8**
butter **16**
buy *v* **14**
by (by bus) **18**
Bye **10**

C
cafe **5**
cafeteria **10**
cake **10**
Cambridge **8**
cameraman **2**
Canada **7**
Canadian **7**
Can I have . . . **10**
canteen **19**
car **7**
car park **6**
centre **6**
cheap **6**
cheers! **12**
cheese **14**
child **11**
children **11**
chips **16**
chocolate **10, 15**
church **16**
cigarette **14**
cinema **5**
class **12**
classical music **11**
classroom **9**
clean *v* **9**
close *v* **13**
closed **14**
clothes **11**
club **12**
coca-cola **11**
coffee **10**
cold **9**
college **19**
come (came) *v* **17**
comfortable **9**
congratulations **4**
cook *v* **11**
cooking **11**
cost **18**
country **6**
cup **10**
cycle **18**

D
dance *v* **12**
date **15**
day **14**
Dear **9**
December **15**
detective story **11**
diary **17**

different **15**
dining room **9**
dinner **14**
do **2**
doctor **3**
documentary film **16**
dog **11**
don't laugh! **16**
don't worry **10**
door **14**
do some shopping **14**
do the ironing **19**
double **4**
downstairs **9**
drink **12**
drink *v* **14**
drive *v* **11**

E
each **10**
early **19**
east **8**
easy **7**
eat *v* **14**
Edinburgh **8**
egg **14**
eight **4**
eighteen **9**
eighth **15**
eighty **10**
eleven **9**
engineer **3**
England **7**
English **7**
envelope **14**
evening **13**
exactly **8**
excuse me! **1**
expensive **6**

F
factory **19**
fairly **6**
family **15**
father **7**
February **15**
fifteen **7**
fifth **15**
fifty **10**
film **13**
film director **2**
find *v* **16**
fine thanks! **17**
finish *v* **13**
first **15**
fish **14**
five **4**
flat **4**
flight **13**
flower **15**

fly **19**
food **9**
football **17**
foreign **19**
forty **10**
four **4**
fourteen **9**
fourth **15**
free **17**
Friday **15**
friend **3**
from **7**
fruit **14**

G
garage **9**
garden **9**
get *v* **11**
get to **18**
get up **19**
girl **7**
give *v* **15**
glass **10**
go home **16**
good **12**
Goodbye **3**
Good morning **4**
go out for . . . **15**
go to **15**
go to bed **19**
go to sleep **16**
go to work **19**
guess *v* **7**

H
half **11**
hall **9**
Happy Birthday **15**
have **10**
have breakfast **19**
Hello! **3**
her **3**
here **3**
here you are **10**
his **3**
holiday **16**
home **15**
hospital **19**
hostel **6**
hot **9**
hotel **5**
hour **18**
house **9**
housewife **3**
housework **19**
how? **18**
how are you? **17**
How do you do! **2**
however **18**
how far? **18**

WHICH WORD TO USE

The figure in **bold** beside each word tells you in which Unit the word first appears for you to learn it.

Occupations
teacher **1**
journalist **2**
film director **2**
cameraman **2**
secretary **2**
technician **2**
van driver **2**
typist **2**
engineer **3**
housewife **3**
student **3**
doctor **3**

Persons
man **5**
woman **5**
girl **7**
boy **7**
child **11**
children **11**
people **15**

Family relatives
sister **7**
brother **7**
mother **7**
father **7**
parents **8**
children **11**
family **15**
husband **19**
wife **19**

Titles
Mr **1**
Mrs **1**
Miss **1**

Countries and Nationalities
England **7**
English **7**
America **7**
American **7**
Canada **7**
Canadian **7**
Ireland **7**
Irish **7**
Australia **7**
Australian **7**
Italian **12**

Places and Buildings
park **1**
road **1**
station **1**
flat **4**
bank **5**
cinema **5**
hotel **5**

school **5**
office **5**
post office **5**
restaurant **5**
police station **5**
supermarket **5**
cafe **5**
airport **6**
air terminal **6**
centre (city) **6**
shopping centre **6**
car park **6**
bar **6**
hostel **6**
suburb **8**
garden **9**
garage **9**
beach **9**
cafeteria **10**
university **12**
town **12**
club **12**
shop **13**
theatre **16**
church **16**
factory **19**
canteen **19**
hospital **19**
studio **19**
pub **19**
college **19**

Rooms and Furniture
bedroom **4**
room **6**
table **6**
dining room **9**
sitting room **9**
bathroom **9**
kitchen **9**
toilet **9**
hall **9**
garage **9**
classroom **9**
window **14**
door **14**
television **15**

Food, Drink and Meals
food **9**
cup **10**
glass **10**
packet **10**
biscuit **10**
cake **10**
sandwich **10**
coffee **10**
tea **10**
water **10**
milk **10**

wine **10**
beer **10**
orange juice **10**
chocolate **10, 15**
sugar **11**
lemon **11**
whisky **11**
coca-cola **11**
drink **12**
eat *v* **14**
apple **14**
orange **14**
egg **14**
potato **14**
tomato **14**
fruit **14**
bread **14**
meat **14**
fish **14**
cheese **14**
vegetables **14**
menu **14**
lunch **14**
supper **14**
dinner **14**
meal **15**
chips **16**
butter **16**
toast **16**
lunchtime **17**
breakfast **19**
pint **19**

Shops and Shopping
supermarket **5**
shopping centre **6**
price **6**
cheap **6**
expensive **6**
pound **9**
how much? **9**
pence **10**
can I have **10**
here you are **10**
shop **13**
do some shopping **14**

Transport and Traffic
road **1**
station **1**
van driver **2**
car park **6**
taxi **6**
bus **6**
airport **6**
drive **11**
train **13**
plane **13**
flight **13**
platform **13**

ticket **14**
rush-hour **18**
bicycle **18**
petrol **18**
mile **18**
kilometre **18**
traffic **18**
accident **18**

Travel and Holidays
map **5**
tourist **6**
airport **6**
air terminal **6**
taxi **6**
hostel **6**
river **6**
country **6**
beach **9**
sea **9**
sightseeing **11**
sunbathing **11**
suitcase **14**
ticket **14**
postcard **16**
holiday **16**
journey **18**
travel **18**
foreign **20**
language **20**
world **20**
abroad **20**
fly **20**

School
teacher **1**
student **3**
school **11**
learn **11**
write **11**
university **12**
lesson **12**
class **12**
college **19**
study **19**

Time
week **9**
what's the time? **11**
o'clock **11**
past **11**
to **11**
quarter **11**
half **11**
watch **11**
a.m. **13**
p.m. **13**
morning **13**
afternoon **13**
evening **13**
late **13**
what time . . ? **13**
date **15**
today **15**
tomorrow **15**
year **15**

yesterday **16**
last night **16**
last week **16**
weekend **16**
tonight **17**
this evening **17**
lunchtime **17**
minute **18**
hour **18**

Days of the week
Months of the year
(see Unit 15)
Numbers
1–10 *(see Unit 4)*
11–20 *(see Unit 9)*
20–100 *(see Unit 10)*
Ordinals: 1st, 2nd etc. *(see Unit 15)*
double **4**
telephone number **4**
quarter **11**
half **11**
single **13**
how many? **14**
how much? **18**

Weather
temperature **9**
hot **9**
cold **9**
warm **9**
day **14**
beautiful **14**
awful **14**
terrible **14**
lovely **14**

Verbs: Daily routine activities
work **6**
drive **11**
smoke **11**
cook **11**
write **11**
sleep **12**
dance **12**
leave **13**
arrive **13**
start **13**
finish **13**
open **13**
close **13**
buy **14**
do some shopping **14**
eat **14**
pack up **14**
drink **14**
go to **15**
go out for . . **15**
watch (TV) **15**
stay at home **15**
sit (sat) down **16**
go (went) home **16**
go (went) to sleep **16**
come (came) **17**
get to **18**
take **18**

walk **18**
cycle **18**
get (got) up **19**
go to work **19**
go to bed **19**
go home **19**
have (had) breakfast **19**
read (read) the paper **19**
do (did) the housework **19**
do the ironing **19**
do homework **19**
mark (marked) homework **19**
study (studied) **19**
listen (listened) to some music **19**
play (played) some records **19**
work for **19**

Other useful verbs
be (am, is etc) **1**
do **2**
send **4**
want **5**
remember **6**
reserve **6**
meet **7**
guess **7**
look at **7**
live **8**
have **10**
like **11**
think **11**
speak **11**
learn **11**
give **15**
stay **15**
see (saw) **16**
invite (invited) **16**
bring (brought) **17**
cost **18**
take **18**
prefer (preferred) **19**

Useful adjectives
young **5**
nice **5**
cheap **6**
expensive **6**
new **7**
big **9**
hot **9**
cold **9**
warm **9**
clean **9**
tasty **9**
comfortable **9**
red **10**
white **10**
strong **10**
black **11**
good **12**
lonely **12**
short **12**
little **12**
single **13**
return **13**
late **13**

lovely **14**
beautiful **14**
terrible **14**
awful **14**
open **14**
closed **14**
interesting **15**
ill **16**
bored **16**
tired **16**
old **16**
well **17**
free **17**
early **19**

Adverbs
over there **1**
here **3**
fairly **6**
exactly **8**
now **8**
very **9**
soon **12**

quickly **12**
quite **16**
always **18**
usually **18**
sometimes **18**
often **18**
never **18**
ever **18**

Prepositions
next to **5**
behind **5**
in front of **5**
opposite **5**
near **5**
from **7**
in **8**
north **8**
south **8**
east **8**
west **8**
with **11**
to **11**

at **14**
on **15**
after **17**
before **17**
by **18**

Question words
What **1**
Where **1**
How much **9**
What time **13**
How many **14**
When **15**
Which **14**
Who **16**
How **18**
How far **18**
How long **18**

Conjunctions
and **3**
or **5**
but **8**
then **14**

CLOUDSONGS

1 Cloudsongs

. . . . these are my cloudsongs
Songs with simple rhymes
These are my cloudsongs
            Cloudsongs
(Songs with simple lines)
These are the songs
I sing with friends
My beginnings
And my ends
They are my music
My magic.

My beginnings
And my ends
They are my music
My magic
These are my songs
These are my songs
Cloudsongs are my songs.

I am, you are

I am the sun
You are the sunlight
You are the moon
I am the moonlight
I am the stars
You are space
I am time, time, time
I am time.

You are the sun
I am the sunshine
We are one
I am yours
You are mine.
I am the sun
You are the sunshine
We are one
I am yours
You are mine.

I am the night
You are the night time
I am the day
You are the day time
I am the rain
You are the wind
I am time, time, time
I am time.

You are the sun . . .

2 Number Seven

Seven . . six . . five . . four . . three . .
   two . . one . . take off!

Seven is my favourite number
Seven is the number for me
He's on flight one two seven
On a Boeing seven four seven

And he's only seven hours away from me
Only seven hours away from me.

Good morning, hallo darling,
Is that one three five eight nine?
Good morning, hallo darling,
Yes, it's me, I'm on the line.
Good morning, hallo darling,
The sky above is blue.
Good morning, hallo darling,
Goodbye and I love you.

Seven is my favourite number . . .

Good morning London Airport,
Flight one two seven on the line,
Good morning London Airport,
Up here the weather's fine.
Good morning London Airport,
The sky above is blue,
Good morning London Airport,
Good bye, good luck, thank you.

Seven is my favourite number . . . . . .

3 Luba's

Luba's, Luba's
L.U.B.A. Luba's
Luba's is the best bistro in town.
Luba's, Luba's
L.U.B.A. Luba's
Luba's is the best bistro in town.
It's near the park
Behind the school
And opposite the swimming pool
Luba's is the best bistro in town.

Go there! Go there!
People say, 'Oh, go there!'
Luba's is the best bistro in town.
It's near the park . . . .

Where is, where is
Where is Luba's bistro?
Where is the best bistro in town?
It's near the park . . . .

Tell me, tell me
Where is Luba's bistro?
Where is the best bistro in town?
It's near the park . . . .

4   Would you like some information?

I'm a perfect, very perfect
Tourist Courier and Guide
And every summer, every morning
I am always at your side . . .

Would you like some information?
Would you like a hotel room?
Would you like a reservation?
You would? Oh, good! How soon?

I'm a perfect, very perfect
Tourist Courier and Guide

And I welcome all the tourists every
   morning,
I take them on a bus
And with very little fuss
I give them information
Every morning.

Would you like . . . .

But I'm a lonely, very lonely
Tourist Courier and Guide
And I welcome all the tourists every
   morning
But then I say goodbye
And they all say goodbye
And I'm alone again, alone again,
   alone again . . .

Would you like . . . .

5   Let's talk

Let's talk
Let's talk about it gently—you and I
You and I, let's talk
And confidently say
'We are in love,
We are in love together now
So much in love,
So much in love forever now
Just you and I,
Just you and I,'
Let's talk.

You and I have different skins
But no-one knows where love begins—
Mysteriously.
All right, let's talk about the future
   now
Talk seriously about the future now
Let's tell the world we're hand in glove
Let's tell the world that we're in love—

Let's talk . . .

6   Sounds of the city

Listen—hear it
Look—and see it
Touch—and feel it
Inside your brain . . .

Oh I love the shadows of the city
Oh I love the city lights
Oh I love the sound of singing
When the city comes alive at night.
The city comes alive at night.

Come and hear the sounds of the city
Come and feel the rhythm of the trains
Come and see the sunset in the evening
Flashing on a million window panes.

Oh I love the sounds of the city
Oh I love the rhythm of the trains
Oh I love the sunset in the evening
Flashing on a million window panes.

Do you like the shadows of the city?
Do you like the city lights?
Do you hear the sound of singing
When the city comes alive at night?

Oh the city comes alive at night
And it's shining like a million
Shining like a million, shining like a
    million
Shining like a million stars.

Listen—hear it . . .

SIDE 2

7 All the time

And I love him
As he loves me
And I need him
As he needs me
And I want him
As he wants me
All the time.

And when he plays all day
In that Rock Cafe
I love him all the time
He's a music man
This man of mine.
He sings the blues
And he plays guitar
And I really love
The things he does—
This man of mine
This man of mine's a star.

And I love him . . .

8 Johnny come home

Oh, Johnny, please come back to me
You know you mean the world to me
Oh, Johnny, please come home again
Oh, Johnny, please come home again.

Johnny left home on the midnight
    train
Why did Johnny leave home?
He bought a ticket on the midnight
    train
Why did Johnny leave home?

But Johnny was young just out of
    school
He only wanted to see
What life was like in the great big city
Johnny wanted to be free.

Oh, Johnny, please come back to me . . .

Johnny was cold. The snow was falling
Why did Johnny leave home?
They found him there some time next
    morning
Why did Johnny leave home?

But Johnny was young, just out of
    school
His mother started to cry
It seems such a shame, such a tragic
    shame
Johnny why did you die?

Oh, Johnny, please come back to me . . .

9 By train

Two men, two jobs
They both start work at nine
One man always gets there late
But the other man's always on time:

'I always leave my home at eight
And I always arrive at nine
In the summer sun and the winter rain
I always go to work by train
I always go by train.'

Two men, two jobs
They both start work at nine
One man always goes by car
But he's never there on time.
His boss says 'Why don't you
    sometimes try
To get to work on time?'

(And the other man says) . . .
'I always leave my home at eight
And I always arrive at nine
In the summer sun and the winter rain
I always, always go by train
I always—No, not sometimes go by
    train.'

10 Where did you go?

And we are strangers now
Once we were friends
We are not lovers now . . .

Where did you go?
What did you do?
And did you know that I was true?
Why did you leave?
Why did you leave me
All alone, all alone?

Why did you go away from home?
Why did you leave me all alone?
Why did you leave me
With my memories and dreams?
Where did you meet that other man?

Why did you show me that I am
Just nothing in the world
Without you.

Where did you go? . . . .

11 Lovely day

I get up in the morning
When the sun gets up
I drink my morning coffee
From my favourite cup.

And I say 'Hey! Hey!
It's a lovely day
It's a lovely day
Yes, it's a marvellous
And wonderful
And absolutely beautiful
A fabulous day . . . .
Hey, hey, it's a lovely day
A marvellous day
A wonderful day
An absolutely beautiful day.'

The postman rings the doorbell
When it's eight o'clock
The milkman leaves the milk
And gives the door a knock. ('*Morning*
    miss!')

And I say 'Hey! Hey!

12 Cloudsongs
(This song begins as **Lovely Day** ends)

These are my cloudsongs
Songs with simple lines
These are my cloudsongs
        Cloudsongs
These are the songs I sing with friends
My beginnings
And my ends
They are my music
My magic
My beginnings
And my ends
They are my music
My magic.

I sing of life
And sing of living
Sing of gifts
And sing of giving
Of simple things
Like kisses in the rain
I sing of love
And present laughter
I sing of time, time, time . . . .

These are my cloudsongs . . .